Adventurous Leadership: Leadership Analogies from the Pacific Crest Trail

David Wilson

Published by David Wilson, 2024.

While every precaution has been taken in the preparation of this book, the publisher assumes no responsibility for errors or omissions, or for damages resulting from the use of the information contained herein.

ADVENTUROUS LEADERSHIP: LEADERSHIP ANALOGIES FROM THE PACIFIC CREST TRAIL

First edition. August 18, 2024.

ISBN: 979-8227206428

Written by David Wilson.

Adventurous Leadership

At 51, after a bankruptcy and a divorce, David Wilson set out to thru-hike all 2,650 miles of the Pacific Crest Trail. He wanted to get away from the grind, see what he was still made of, and figure out who he wanted to be next. Five months later, he had walked from the Mexican border to Canada—700 miles of desert, the Sierra Nevada, the highest peak in the lower 48, and right through one of the worst wildfire seasons California had ever seen. Along the way he picked up a trail's worth of lessons about leadership—the kind you only get when you're tired, dirty, hungry, and have nothing left to do but keep walking. This is his story, and the leadership analogies he carried home from it.

INTRODUCTION

"Life is either a daring adventure or nothing at all" – Helen Keller

The word "trek" can be defined as "to make one's way arduously," and indeed, the leadership journey can be just that—arduous. Leadership is filled with adversity, success, fun, challenges, wins, losses, and disappointments. It can be a wild roller coaster. My advice: embrace your role as a leader and learn as much as you can. While you may never fully master it, you can certainly become one of the greats.

During my time on the Pacific Crest Trail (PCT), I frequently heard from fellow hikers of all types, "the trail is an analogy for life." I couldn't agree more. The trail offers an incredible number of analogies that also apply to leadership. My goal in writing this book is to share some of those leadership analogies with you while providing a glimpse into life on the PCT. I hope this book will aid you on your leadership journey and inspire you to get outside and live life adventurously.

At the age of 51, I decided to undertake a "thru-hike" of the PCT. For those unfamiliar with the term, "thru-hiking" means starting at one end and hiking continuously all the way to the other. The PCT is a 2,650-mile trail that stretches from Campo, California, to the Canadian border. Thru-hiking the PCT typically takes about five to six months of continuous hiking. Each year, roughly 800 people attempt to complete the PCT, and only about 60% succeed. The trail begins with 700 miles of desert hiking, transitions into the high-altitude Sierra Nevada mountains, continues through Northern California, traverses the beautiful landscapes of Oregon, and concludes with the particularly challenging section in Washington.

So, why did I embark on this journey? That's the big question every hiker is asked, both by fellow hikers and by friends and family. "Why are you doing this?" or "Is this your mid-life crisis?" Even I had to ask myself why I had chosen to undertake such an endeavor.

Part of me simply wanted to escape reality for a while—escape work, bills, traffic, relationships, and the constant expectations others had of me. I wanted to get away from it all. I had grown tired of feeling like my entire life revolved around my job. I was lucky if I could find even two hours a week to get outside, hike, or mountain bike without work interrupting. It got to the point where I thought, This can't be what life is supposed to be like. There must be more. God created so many wonderful places, and I feared I'd never see them.

I spent more time in my car dealing with traffic and even more time inside some work building, only to go home to rest for the next workday. The thought of working like this until I died held no appeal for me. I wanted to experience something more while I still had some youth left. There are so many wonders in nature I wanted to see, and I was beginning to worry I never would.

The other reason I undertook this journey was that I wanted to discover something within myself. At 50, I already knew a lot about myself. I knew I was a hard worker, organized, compassionate, friendly, determined, and occasionally indecisive or prone to procrastination. But I sensed there was more, something deep inside me that had been numbed by "the world"—the grind of work, materialism, and societal expectations. I needed to awaken that part of myself, and I believed the best way to do that was to immerse myself in something completely uncomfortable and extremely difficult, something that would challenge me mentally as much as physically while pulling me away from "the world" for an extended time.

For years, I had tried to write a book on leadership. As a young leader, I had been inspired by Ken Blanchard's books. A friend introduced me to *The One Minute Manager*, which opened my eyes to how little I knew about leading people. I had served as a Drill Sergeant in the Army Reserves and assumed the leadership training I received in the military was all I needed to succeed in the business world. However, as I progressed through Blanchard's books and moved on to works by authors like John Maxwell, Patrick Lencioni, and Spencer Johnson, I realized how much more there was to learn about leadership.

Over time, I also came to realize that very few of the leaders around me put any effort into developing their leadership skills and knowledge. As I continued reading and applying what I learned, I found myself teaching others what I thought were basic leadership principles. Teaching younger leaders became my favorite part of the job. Eventually, I began to believe that I could write a valuable leadership book.

However, every time I tried, my writing felt dry and unoriginal. I didn't think I had anything new or interesting to offer. Now, after completing a life-changing adventure filled with rich leadership analogies, I finally have the material I need to write the book I've been wanting to write for years.

To get a great visual experience of life on the PCT, please scan the random QR codes that will take you to a specific YouTube video related to that part of my journey.

CHAPTER 1
PLANNING FOR SUCCESS

"The soul grows by subtraction, not addition" – Henry David Thoreau

I can vividly recall the first day of this incredible new adventure. It was 1:00 p.m. when I was dropped off at the Southern Terminus in Campo, California. The heat hit me like a wall. Though the temperature was only 80 degrees, it felt much hotter in the dry desert air. Standing there, just 30 feet away from the imposing Mexican border wall, surrounded by nothing but dirt, cactus, and patches of dry brown grass, I was filled with a sense of sobering reality. Yet, despite this stark environment, an overwhelming feeling of excitement surged through me. I wasn't alone in that moment—three other hikers had just arrived as well. We all shared in the excitement, laughing, taking pictures, and chatting about the journey that lay ahead. We stood on the Southern Terminus monument for our customary pictures, then after a bit more conversation, each of us loaded up our packs and started walking. I'll never forget how heavy my pack felt—it was easily 10-15 pounds heavier than it needed to be. As a "rookie" thru-hiker, I had made the mistake of thinking that my strength and fitness would carry me through the hardships. With about 7 million steps ahead of me, I reassured myself with the mantra, "One step and one day at a time."

Those first few miles are burned into my memory. The heat was unrelenting, the sound of grasshoppers filled the air, and the crunch of the dry dirt under my boots was a constant reminder of the harshness of the terrain. All the while, the thought kept bouncing around in my head: "Are you really doing this?" Starting a 2,650-mile journey felt surreal, almost as though I was just out on a simple 10-mile day hike. The magnitude of what I was undertaking hadn't yet settled in. Around three miles into the hike, I found a good spot to take my first break at some railroad tracks. There was a large rock, perfectly shaped to rest my pack on. By then, my shoulders were already aching. I took off my pack, chugged some Gatorade, and snapped a few photos to capture the moment. Soon after, a train rolled by with a few passengers on board, and to my surprise, some of them leaned out and shouted, "Good luck!" It was a special moment—hearing their encouragement filled me with pride. Clearly, they knew what I was attempting, and I felt a sense of pride in that acknowledgment. As I stood there, an older man came up behind me, and we struck up a conversation. I noticed his pack was much lighter than mine. That was the first moment I started questioning if I had overpacked or underprepared for what lay ahead.

Later that evening, after covering roughly 7 miles, I met up with him again, along with another hiker. The three of us decided to camp in the same area. River, the other hiker, had already passed out in her tent when I arrived. David, the older man, and I chatted for a bit, setting up our tents, preparing quick dinners, and then crashing for the night. The exhaustion from the day's hike had caught up with all of us. The next morning, we each set out at different times. I overheard David and River talking about Lake Morena, a place I didn't even know existed at the time. That day brought intense challenges—there was relentless heat, no shade, and several hills full of loose, chunky rocks. Every time I found a patch of shade, I took the opportunity to remove my socks and shoes, drying them in the sun, rubbing my feet with powder, and drinking as much water as I could afford to. However, it wasn't long before I realized I was running dangerously low on water and had to start rationing it carefully.

Using the Guthook app on my phone, which showed the trail's route, water sources, and campsites, I saw that there was a water source at Hauser Creek a few miles ahead. By the time I arrived, I was desperate for water. I found River setting up camp near the creek, which had a few good spots for camping and some much-needed shade. However, the water itself was stagnant and looked unappealing. Exhausted, sweaty, and thirsty, I climbed down into the creek bed and filled a two-liter bag with the murky water. I filtered it twice and added iodine tablets to be safe, knowing full well that it wasn't going to taste great. After a brief rest, I pressed on but quickly realized that the two liters I'd collected wouldn't be enough. I needed more water for dinner and the next morning, but I had to make do with what I had. Dehydration was already setting in. I couldn't make it to my planned campsite, so I decided to stop at a tiny spot just two feet off the trail. Before setting up camp, I went to relieve myself and realized I hadn't urinated in over 11 hours—a sure sign that I had pushed my dehydration too far. Waking up in the middle of the night with a dry mouth,

I took a small, unsatisfying sip of the iodine-treated water. The willpower it took not to gulp it all down in one go was immense.

When I woke up the next morning, I had a terrible case of cottonmouth. That was the moment I knew I had to get serious about planning. "Winging it" wasn't going to cut it for this 2,650-mile journey. I needed to plan out where I was going, where the water sources were, and how far I'd have to go between campsites. The Guthook app provided invaluable information—not just about the trail, but from other hikers who left comments about water availability, campsites, and upcoming towns. From that day forward, I adopted a 48-hour rolling plan. Each night, I made a plan for the next two days, mapping out water sources, campsites, and resupply points. This strategy gave me confidence and structure. Soon, other hikers began noticing and asking me how I was planning my days, and I was more than happy to share my approach.

One of the most important lessons I'd learned during my time in the Army was that failed missions often came down to the "4 Ps"—Piss Poor Prior Planning. As a leader, you're responsible not just for yourself but for the success of your team, and that success is directly tied to how well you plan. I've often heard young leaders say, "I don't have time to plan." But we all have the same amount of time—it's just a matter of how you use it and what you prioritize. Planning may seem like it takes too much time, but in reality, good, simple planning saves time in the long run.

Take Tim, for example, a General Manager at a restaurant who never plans. He arrives at work late, jumps into the chaos of the day, and spends the whole time reacting—placing rushed food orders, scrambling to cover for sick employees, and dealing with unexpected deliveries. Tim works hard, but his lack of planning leads to a stressful environment, unhappy employees, and poor service for his customers. Though things may occasionally work out, it doesn't take many bad days before employees leave and customers stop coming.

Contrast that with Andrew, another General Manager. He spends just 15 minutes each week forecasting sales and writing schedules. Every Sunday evening, he takes another 15 minutes to review his team's availability and address potential issues. When he sees that Brian, who's scheduled to open on Monday, is still sick, he takes 10 minutes to find a replacement. Andrew arrives at work prepared, and the day runs smoothly—his team is happy, the customers are satisfied, and he leaves the day with a sense of accomplishment.

These aren't hypothetical scenarios—they happen all the time. Leaders like Tim, who refuse to plan, often lead their teams into unnecessary stress and burnout. They're willing to put in the physical effort but neglect the mental work that true leadership requires. In contrast, leaders like Andrew recognize that a little mental effort in planning can go a long way in creating a smoother, more successful operation.

As a leader, it's essential to take planning seriously, not just for yourself but for the success of your team. If planning doesn't come naturally to you, find someone in your organization who excels at it and learn from them. Just like the hikers I helped who weren't natural planners but made the effort to succeed, you too can become a more effective leader by embracing the value of preparation. It doesn't have to be complicated, but it will make a world of difference for your team and your overall work-life balance. When your work thrives, so does your personal life.

CHAPTER 2
REINVENTING YOURSELF

Waking up at 3:30 a.m. on my first solo night in the desert, I was overwhelmed by the serene beauty surrounding me—the vast expanse of the night sky, the profound silence, and the crisp, refreshing air. I had purposefully left the rain cover off my tent, which gave me an uninterrupted view of the stars. They shimmered like diamonds scattered across the sky, and I lay there, mesmerized. This moment was everything I had envisioned and more. I was completely alone, miles away from civilization, in the heart of the desert, and I relished every second of it. Surprisingly, the fear I had anticipated before embarking on this adventure never came. Instead, I felt an overwhelming sense of peace, accomplishment, and happiness, tempered only by a hint of fatigue.

The only real issue was that my water supply was running dangerously low. I had barely enough to make a single cup of coffee and take two small sips before I began my 5-mile trek to Lake Morena. My morning routine was a comforting ritual that grounded me: Bible reading, enjoying my coffee, a quick bowl of oatmeal, stretching, a set of pushups, and packing up my gear. That morning, as part of documenting my journey, I recorded a brief video for my YouTube channel, summarizing my first episode on the trail. Once I finished, I laced up my trail runners, shouldered my heavy pack, and set off once more on the trail.

Night hiking quickly became one of my favorite parts of the experience. It allowed me to escape the brutal desert heat, marvel at the splendor of the night sky, feel the cool air on my skin, and revel in the solitude. It was thrilling to be out there in the desert, not merely surviving, but truly thriving. This new lifestyle made me realize that happiness didn't require material possessions. The joy I felt out there was pure and raw, unlike anything I had ever experienced before—something that no car, house, money, or clothing could ever provide. As I took my first steps into the darkness that morning, I thought to myself, "I can finish this journey." Even though I was only a couple of days in, I felt confident. I had already survived the tough first days, so why not continue for another 178 miles?

Though my optimistic attitude had sometimes led me into trouble in the past, this time, I was sure it would guide me toward success. I could feel it in my bones.

As I neared Lake Morena, my thirst became almost unbearable. Those two small sips of water over the last five miles weren't even close to enough. When I finally arrived at the large campsite, I made a beeline for the water spigot. I filled up two bottles and collapsed onto a nearby bench, drinking the cool, refreshing water in pure relief. That simple act of rehydrating felt like a triumph. I had made it there on my own, and the sense of pride was immense. To my delight, I discovered that the campsite had real bathrooms, running water, comfortable campsites, and even nearby stores.

Although I had initially only planned to refill my water and take a short break before getting back on the trail, I decided to give myself the rest of the day off to recover and relax.

A few hours later, David, River, and some other hikers I had met along the way showed up, and we all agreed to stay the day at the campsite. Together, we walked to a local restaurant, where we indulged in burgers, fries, soda, and ice cream. It was a wonderful experience, sharing stories about the trials we had faced, the mistakes we had made, and the aches and pains our bodies were enduring. After setting up my tent, I treated myself to a camp shower, which operated on a timer based on how many quarters you had. Since I didn't have many, I knew I had to make the time count. I even brought some of my dirty clothes into the shower with me, washing them as I cleaned myself. Slowly but surely, I was falling in love with the simplicity of this life.

While at the campsite, we had the pleasure of meeting a Trail Angel named Tricia. Trail Angels are incredibly kind people who dedicate their time and resources to supporting hikers on long trails. Tricia treated us to pizza, wine, burgers, and beer. We spent the evening laughing, swapping stories about our lives, and enjoying the beauty of the surroundings. It was during this time that we also began discussing "trail names"—the nicknames that hikers adopt for the duration of their journey. While it might seem like a small detail, fully embracing trail culture and leaving behind the norms of the conventional world is a key part of the experience. David became known as "Walk-About," River took on the name "Soul Sister," and I was still waiting for my trail name to be chosen.

Looking back on those early days of the trail, I have nothing but fond memories. I was free from the pressures and complexities of the outside world, living a life that was simple, joyful, and beautiful in its own way. Despite the hardships, I thrived on the challenges, and the sense of accomplishment from overcoming them felt good. We all embraced the early stages of the trail with a sense of wonder and anticipation, knowing that the experience would change us in profound ways. Building relationships came easily out there because we were all facing the same struggles—there were no socio-economic barriers, no distinctions between rich and poor, cool or nerdy. We were all just tired, hungry, dirty, and sore, yet we found joy in the smallest pleasures of life.

In the "real world," there are moments when we feel the urge to change, to become someone different from who we are now. Whether it's pursuing a new career, striving to be a better spouse or parent, taking on a new role at work, or adopting a healthier lifestyle, it takes an incredible amount of courage to take that first step. Sometimes, it's a major life event, or even something as simple as a birthday, that makes us reflect on who we want to become. But courage alone isn't enough. Real change requires discipline, determination, planning, and perseverance.

At some point, there comes a shift in your mindset. You stop saying, "This is who I want to be," and instead, you declare, "This is who I am." It's at that moment that you start taking the necessary steps to truly become that person. You begin pursuing a new career, taking on that new role, striving to be a better spouse or parent, or embracing a more adventurous lifestyle. You stop wasting time contemplating who you want to become and simply start being that person.

From my own experience, the journey of becoming someone new follows several distinct stages:

1. **Excitement:** Starting something new is always exciting. Your motivation is at an all-time high, and you're full of energy. This phase is crucial because that initial adrenaline carries you through the first steps. When I began my PCT journey, I was thrilled, posing with my gear, snapping photos at the southern terminus, and basking in the encouragement from family and friends.

2. **Difficulty:** Eventually, reality sets in, and you're faced with the challenges of your new endeavor. The excitement fades, and the hard work becomes apparent. This hit me quickly on the PCT when the thrill wore off, and I faced the harsh reality of the trek ahead.

3. **Arrogance:** This stage can be tricky. After a few early successes, you may start feeling overconfident, thinking, "I've got this all figured out!" I've encountered this before, particularly in mountain biking. After a few easy rides, I thought I was ready for a more challenging trail, only to find myself taking multiple tumbles in quick succession.

4. **Humility:** Eventually, something humbling happens that reminds you just how much you still have to learn. For me, it was the realization that I had completely mismanaged my water supply. The

experience of rationing water in the desert reminded me that I didn't have everything figured out after all.

5. **Confidence:** Finally, after a period of struggle and growth, you reach a point where you truly feel capable. You've faced challenges, learned from them, and gained confidence in your abilities. For me, this came when I mastered the art of planning my water sources and understood the demands of the trail. I started learning from other hikers and recognized that I could absolutely complete the journey. That's when I knew with certainty, "I've got this!"

These stages are common in any challenging experience, whether it's hiking the PCT or pursuing personal growth. Understanding that these phases will come can help you prepare mentally to face each one as it arrives.

CHAPTER 3
TRUDGING IS INEVITABLE

Leaving Julian, California, turned out to be much harder than I had anticipated. This charming little town in San Diego County, with a population of roughly 1,800, is officially recognized as a California Historical Landmark. Famous for its apple pies and annual apple festival, Julian has a quaint, nostalgic feel that makes it hard to leave once you've experienced its unique charm. I was lucky enough to find a place to stay at the Julian Gold Rush Hotel, as the town was packed for the weekend. The more affordable rooms were already booked, so I ended up in a separate, more expensive cottage that was located away from the main hotel building. At the time, I didn't care about the cost; I was just thrilled to sleep in a real bed and take a hot bath after days on the trail.

Stepping into the upstairs barn-style cottage immediately brought back memories of my grandma's house. The decor was filled with touches of the past—doilies under the lamps, floral-patterned curtains and bedding, and a classic white clawfoot bathtub that beckoned me to relax. I quickly filled the tub with steaming water, dropped my gear, and sank into what felt like the most glorious bath of my life. After soaking and scrubbing for about an hour, I laughed when I noticed the water had turned an alarming shade of brown. It was both funny and a reminder of just how dirty I'd become from days out on the trail.

After getting cleaned up and dressed, I walked into town to meet up with Jared, who hadn't yet earned a trail name, and BlackMagic. We made our way to the iconic Mom's Pie House, where all Pacific Crest Trail (PCT) thru-hikers are treated to a free slice of apple pie. The town was teeming with other hikers, their weathered backpacks lined up outside of restaurants and shops while they restocked their food supplies, grabbed a meal, or browsed for new gear. I loved being part of this lively hiker community. There was something special about being one of the "dirty hobos" and sharing the experience with others who understood the challenges of life on the trail. I remember meeting a young couple that day, both probably in their early twenties. The guy had a scruffy beard, and the girl sported long, dirty dreadlocks, unshaven legs, and a carefree "hippy chic" look.

We struck up a conversation, and they asked if they could use the shower in my hotel room, explaining they couldn't afford a place of their own. Without a second thought, I agreed. The connection between hikers is difficult to explain—there's an unspoken bond that forms from shared experiences. I'm ashamed to admit that in my everyday life, I might have ignored or even judged them based on their appearance. After they cleaned up, we hung out on the balcony of my cottage, swapping stories about our lives back home. They were around the same age as my kids, which stirred a natural desire in me to help them out.

Later that evening, I walked them back into town, bought them dinner, and wished them well as they continued their journey. As we parted ways, they suggested I adopt the trail name "Night Ranger" because of my fondness for night hiking. I loved it immediately and proudly accepted the name as my new trail identity.

The following morning, I woke up feeling completely refreshed. After enjoying the hotel's complimentary breakfast, I packed my gear and prepared to head back to the trail. But the thought of strapping on my heavy backpack, hitchhiking to the trailhead, and hiking in the scorching desert heat weighed heavily on my mind. The first few miles were tough—an unrelenting uphill climb under a blistering sun. My body felt sluggish, probably from the unhealthy food I had indulged in the night before. I had stomach cramps, labored breathing, and aches all over. I was tempted to turn back and take another day off in Julian, but I resisted the urge and pressed on, determined to keep moving forward.

It felt like the entire day was one long, uphill slog. As the sun beat down on me, my energy levels plummeted. After about five grueling hours, I stumbled upon a small, shaded area—the first one I had seen in miles. I quickly unloaded my pack, peeled off my shoes and socks, and sat down to drink some water and have lunch. I laid my socks out in the sun to dry, reclined, and tried to take a nap. While I didn't actually sleep, I rested for about 30 minutes before reluctantly getting back on my feet and continuing along the trail. My motivation was at an all-time low. I just wanted the day to be over. The scenery was bleak, the heat oppressive, and the never-ending climb exhausting. It was the first time on the trail that I truly thought, "Just keep your head down and trudge forward."

Eventually, I came across a small, isolated camping spot about ten feet off the trail. It was a flat patch of sand surrounded by large brown boulders, offering a stunning view of the desert mountains. Exhausted, I set up camp and dug out a couple of oranges I had brought from Julian. I was running low on water, so the oranges were a refreshing and much-needed source of hydration. As I sat on a rock, completely alone, I wished for some company. The solitude and isolation were weighing on me, and I was thankful the day had finally come to an end.

The next morning, I woke to find the trail cold and windy. My mood hadn't improved, and the thought of hiking into the harsh weather was daunting. After my usual morning routine of Bible reading, coffee, oatmeal, stretching, and pushups, I put on my earbuds, cranked up some music, and started packing. It was surreal to think that just the day before, I had been baking in the desert heat, and now I was bundled up in all of my cold-weather gear.

That morning's hike was challenging. The trail was narrow and sloped, which caused my left foot to repeatedly roll outward, sending sharp, shooting pains up my ankle. After a few hours of this, I finally found shelter from the wind behind a large rock. I rubbed my aching ankle, made some coffee, and had a snack. As I sat there, I prayed for strength and reflected on how much the trail mirrored life—especially when things weren't going smoothly. Sometimes, all you can do is keep your head down, say a prayer, and push through, just as I had to do on that tough day.

As the sun slowly climbed higher into the sky, my spirits began to lift. I started to feel a sense of accomplishment for enduring such a difficult stretch. The trail had thrown everything it had at me over the past 24 hours, but I was still standing, still moving forward.

This experience reminded me of how life and work can be equally demanding. Whether it's a personal relationship or a professional challenge, there will be moments when you feel like giving up. But it's important to realize that everyone faces those moments of doubt. That's when you need to "put your head down" and keep going. By "putting your head down," I don't mean ignoring your responsibilities or blindly rushing through tasks. Rather, it's about adopting a mindset of persistence—of rolling up your sleeves and pushing forward despite the difficulties.

If you're truly committed to the process, you must accept that sometimes trudging through is necessary. That's the phase I find myself in now, back in the "real world" and in the grind of everyday work. After experiencing the freedom of the trail, it's been incredibly hard to readjust to life in the "work world." The restaurant business has been particularly challenging since my return. In fact, writing this chapter feels almost hypocritical because, right now, I don't feel like trudging—I feel like throwing my hands up, saying "screw this," and disappearing from society again. But disappearing isn't an option. I know I have to keep going, even when the results aren't immediate. I have to keep putting one foot in front of the other, moving forward, and staying committed to the process.

Ask anyone who's been married for 25 years or more if they've had to trudge, and they'll almost certainly say, "yes."

This principle is one of the most valuable lessons I encountered both on the trail and in life. Great leaders don't quit when things get tough. They find ways to improve the situation, lead by example, and continue to trudge forward.

CHAPTER 4
APPRECIATE THE SMALL THINGS

During this section of the hike, I found myself battling the relentless desert heat day after day, spending countless hours trekking through dry, sun-scorched terrain with very little shade in sight. Despite the brutal conditions, there was an undeniable beauty in the vast solitude of the desert, and I found myself appreciating much of it. Still, there were days when the heat was unbearable, and those stretches of the hike were far from easy. I vividly recall moments when the temperature soared, forcing me to stop for a break whenever I spotted even the tiniest patch of shade. Often, these brief moments of respite were right along the trail, where there was barely enough space to drop my pack without blocking the path for other hikers. But no matter how small or awkward the shade, it was a necessity. I knew that the scorching conditions posed real risks for heat-related illnesses, so I took every opportunity to cool my body down, even if it meant an uncomfortable rest stop.

By this time, I had been hiking through the desert for several days, and the challenges were piling up. Water had become increasingly scarce, and when we did manage to find it, accessing it was often a task in itself. I vividly recall one particular water source that had become a lifeline for all of us, but it was teeming with bees. The water trickled out slowly, and the effort to collect it was made even more frustrating by the swarm of buzzing insects. Despite these discomforts, there was one thought that kept me going: Paradise Café was just around the corner! The café, a little haven about half a mile off the trail, is legendary among hikers for its incredible burgers. After enduring the relentless desert heat and the frustration of scarce water, the thought of arriving at the café lifted my spirits and kept me moving forward. My plan was simple: camp about five miles from the café, wake up early, hike the short distance, and treat myself to a hearty breakfast. Maybe, if I played my cards right, I'd even pack out a burger for lunch later. It's incredible how the simplest pleasures can bring the most excitement when you're out on the trail.

The plan worked perfectly. I woke up early the next morning, and the five-mile hike to the café was a breeze. A group of my fellow hikers arrived at the same time, and we all shared a table, ordered breakfast, and enjoyed some much-needed downtime. We washed up in the restroom, used real toilets—a luxury at that point—and charged our phones while relaxing in actual chairs. As we sat around, sharing stories from the trail, it struck me how, in just a few short days, these fellow hikers had come to feel like family. We laughed and joked as if we had known each other for years. It was an experience that was hard to describe, but I remember it so vividly—a feeling of pure camaraderie that was only possible because of the shared challenges we had faced together.

Leaving the café, I felt completely renewed. My stomach was full, my spirit lifted, and I had a fresh appreciation for the small things in life. The materialistic world that I had once been so immersed in seemed to lose its grip on me, and I reveled in the simplicity of the trail. It wasn't about possessions or comforts anymore; happiness came from a hot cup of coffee, good conversation, and a stack of pancakes. Those little moments were more fulfilling than I could have imagined, and as I hiked away from the café that day, I did a little dance along the trail. I even recorded a quick video, sharing with the world how the most basic things in life had suddenly become the ultimate luxuries. Even now, years later, I look back on that moment and think, *That's what I miss most—the pure joy of being excited and happy about the simple things in life.*

There's something incredibly powerful about that realization. Life is so much richer when you learn to appreciate the simple blessings, as opposed to when you find yourself overwhelmed by an overabundance of unnecessary possessions. In today's world, it's all too easy to get caught up in the pursuit of more—more things, more status, more distractions. But out on the trail, I discovered that the little things, the simple joys, were what truly made life worth living.

As a leader, it's essential to take time to reflect on the small blessings in life. Whether at work or home, acknowledging and giving thanks for the everyday gifts we often overlook can shift your perspective and renew your energy. After all, when you're used to having something, it's easy to take it for granted—especially when the pressures of life push you into survival mode. But the truth is, recognizing the beauty in the small things can help you maintain a positive outlook even when the days are tough.

In over 20 years of leadership, I've seen firsthand how difficult it can be to stay positive in the face of constant challenges. No matter how hard you try to focus on gratitude and optimism, there will be days when the weight of your responsibilities feels overwhelming. But taking even a few moments each day to reflect on the blessings in your life can help you rise above the stress and come out stronger on the other side.

As a leader, your attitude has a direct impact on your team. If they see you handle adversity with grace, determination, and positivity, they'll be inspired to do the same. Conversely, if you're constantly bogged down by frustration, negativity, and anger, that energy will spread, and your team will feel it. That's why it's crucial to remind yourself of the basic blessings in life—because, to someone else, those things might be a luxury.

Consider this: Your spouse loves you, your children are happy, you have a reliable car, your health is good, you enjoyed a perfect cup of coffee this morning, a team member made progress, your boss hasn't been hovering, there's food on the table, and you have clothes on your back. When you start counting your blessings, you'll find that the list is almost endless. And who knows? You might even find yourself dancing down the path of life, just like I did that day on the trail, grateful for the simple luxuries that make every step of the journey worthwhile.

One of the most rewarding aspects of leadership is knowing that you've inspired someone, even if you didn't realize they were paying attention. You may not hear about it right away, but years down the line, someone might reach out and tell you how you influenced their life in a profound way. That's the true legacy of leadership—not in the accolades you collect but in the lives you touch and inspire long after you've moved on.

Learning to appreciate the small blessings will not only make you a more positive leader but also a more resilient one. Gratitude builds strength, both for yourself and for those who look to you for guidance.

CHAPTER 5
GET PAST THAT BOULDER

This morning started off on a high note! The previous days' hikes had been not only breathtakingly beautiful but also relatively easy, so I was in high spirits as I began making my way into the San Jacinto Mountains. The crisp, chilly morning air was refreshing, and I was filled with excitement, knowing I would soon reach the town of Idyllwild for a full "zero day." A full zero day meant I'd arrive in town around 1:00 p.m., check into a hotel, and take an entire day and an extra night to completely rest. Two nights in a hotel felt like a luxurious reward: I would finally get to shower, clean all my gear, resupply my food, charge my electronics, and do my laundry. Plus, I had big plans to indulge in all the unhealthy food I had been craving—pizza, burgers, chips and salsa, ice cream, and a giant box of Fruity Pebbles. By that point, I was thoroughly sick of oatmeal, tuna, and ramen noodles. The thought of real food and a break from the trail was like a beacon pulling me forward.

That morning, everything was going smoothly. The weather was perfect—cool, clear, and invigorating. The trail was absolutely stunning, winding through the mountains, and I was making excellent time. The path ran along the side of a mountain, with a steep, dizzying drop-off to my right that plunged hundreds of feet down. This section of the trail can be especially treacherous in icy conditions, often requiring hikers to use micro-spikes to get traction on the ice-covered rocks. I remembered hearing about a tragic incident that had occurred here a few years back, when a young man lost his life. He had tried to make a short leap from one rock to another without using his micro-spikes, lost his footing, and tragically fell off the cliff. As I passed the small memorial plaque that had been placed in his memory, I knelt and said a prayer for his family, acknowledging the dangers this trail can hold.

A little further along, I encountered a section of the trail that was completely blocked by a massive boulder. I later learned that dynamite had been used to clear the blockage, but at that moment, I had to figure out how to navigate past it. As I approached, I saw another hiker already there, trying to tackle the same problem. His trail name was G-Mac, and though we had never met before, we quickly bonded over the shared challenge of this seemingly impossible obstacle. The trail here was incredibly narrow, only about 18 inches wide, with a steep incline to the left and a steep drop to the right, making it impossible to go around the boulder. Climbing over it appeared to be the only viable option, but it was extremely risky. There was a climbing rope tied around the boulder, presumably placed there to help hikers make the dangerous climb. The drop-off on the right was so severe that a fall would almost certainly be fatal.

G-Mac and I had a decision to make: we could either take the risk of climbing over the boulder or backtrack 12 miles to take an alternate route. Despite the obvious danger, we decided to climb. I carefully double-wrapped the rope around my arm, found a tiny foothold on the cliffside, and gingerly stepped onto it. In that moment, my life was quite literally dependent on that old, worn rope and the narrow foothold beneath my feet. I stood there for about 30 seconds, frozen in place, and then stepped back onto the trail to reconsider my decision. G-Mac and I discussed the situation again, weighing our options, and I made the decision to attempt the climb one more time. This time, I wrapped the rope more securely around my arm, placed my foot on the small foothold, and quickly jumped, pulling myself up onto the boulder.

As soon as I landed on the flat section of the boulder, I became acutely aware of how unbalanced I felt with my 30-pound backpack weighing me down. The flat surface I was standing on was only about three feet wide, and as I tried to sit down, my pack caught on the rock to my left, forcing me to lean dangerously toward the right—toward the sheer drop-off. A surge of panic set in as I realized that retreating was just as dangerous as moving forward. For a few terrifying seconds, I was completely frozen with fear, worried that if I didn't act quickly, my legs would cramp in the awkward position I was in. I knew I needed to move, and fast.

Slowly and cautiously, I shifted my weight into a seated position, making sure my pack didn't pull me off balance. After what felt like an eternity, a quick prayer, and a mental promise to my kids that I would never do something this reckless again, I finally found myself safely seated. I scooted forward on the boulder, carefully inching my way back to the trail. When my feet hit the ground, I was overwhelmed by a mix of relief, adrenaline, and exhilaration. The sense of accomplishment was so intense that, for a moment, I even considered climbing back over the boulder just to experience the rush again! Instead, I offered a sincere prayer of thanks to the Lord for keeping me safe and asked Him to protect G-Mac as well.

Both G-Mac and I successfully navigated the obstacle and continued our hike toward Idyllwild. While we were proud of having overcome the boulder, we both knew it hadn't been the wisest decision. Once again, pride had gotten in the way of common sense, and we had risked our lives when the smarter move would have been to backtrack and take the safer, alternate route.

As a leader, you'll encounter numerous obstacles, some of which will be easy to overcome, while others will seem almost insurmountable. No matter how daunting the challenge may appear, your role is to find a way through, around, over, or under the obstacle. There will be times when the best course of action is to backtrack and find a safer path, but as a leader, you must never simply stop and do nothing. You're responsible for guiding your team forward, even when the way is unclear.

I've worked with many young leaders who haven't yet developed this mindset. When faced with a problem, some freeze and wait for someone else to provide the solution. My wife and I recently went rock climbing with a professional guide, and I found myself hitting mental blocks halfway up the rock. I would think, "There's no way I can reach the top." The rock looked too steep, my leg cramped, and I couldn't find a foothold. But each time, after taking a small step forward, I would discover another foothold, and then another, until eventually, I reached the top. Leadership is much the same—you may not see the whole solution at once, but if you take one step forward, the next step will often reveal itself.

I once worked for a tough boss who had a notoriously aggressive style. When I was struggling with a problem early in my career, he asked me, "If someone had a gun to your head and told you to figure it out, what would you do?" It wasn't the most tactful approach, but it worked. It forced me to think, "If this were a life-or-death situation, how would I solve it?" I can't recall the specific challenge I was facing at the time, but I've never forgotten the analogy. I've since used that same approach when mentoring younger leaders.

As an older leader, I sometimes feel that younger generations lack that same "figure it out" mentality. My father instilled that in me. Growing up, I often found myself in difficult situations, but my dad never bailed me out. I was frustrated at the time, but now I'm grateful for those lessons. They taught me to solve problems on my own. As you gain more experience as a leader, you'll develop that same problem-solving instinct. Sometimes, you'll find the solution on your own, and other times, it will come through collaboration with your team.

Just remember, as a leader, it's not always your responsibility to have the answer right away, but it is your responsibility to lead the effort to solve the problem. Don't approach your boss with an issue unless you've thought about possible solutions first. Talk with your team, brainstorm ideas, and only seek advice from above after you've exhausted your options.

And always think hard about the risk before you decide. Pride will cloud your judgment, like it did mine when I climbed that boulder. If I had set aside my ego and truly assessed the danger, I would have backtracked instead of risking my life. A tiny foothold, an old rope, and a hundred-foot drop weren't worth the gamble. Fortunately, things worked out that time, but next time, I'll choose the safer, more prudent path.

If you ever decide to take a risky solution, be sure to weigh all the factors carefully, put your pride aside, and don't hesitate to backtrack if needed. Leadership is about making wise decisions, not just bold ones.

CHAPTER 6
A JOURNEY TO MINIMALISM

As I made my way down Devil's Slide, a steep and thrilling 1,700-foot descent into the picturesque town of Idyllwild, CA, I was filled with a sense of exhilaration. This wasn't just because I had conquered another challenging section of the Pacific Crest Trail (PCT), but because I was about to enjoy my first true "zero day." Unlike the "nero" (near-zero day) I had taken in Julian, CA, where I rested but still hiked a bit, this would be a full day off with no hiking at all. My legs ached from the miles behind me, and the thought of resting in Idyllwild was incredibly appealing.

G-Mac and I hitched a ride into the tranquil town, which lies nestled in the majestic San Jacinto Mountains of Riverside County. With a population of around 3,800, Idyllwild attracts visitors worldwide, drawn to its scenic beauty and towering trees. It felt worlds away from bigger mountain towns like Big Bear. Idyllwild has hosted a variety of well-known residents over the years, including celebrities like Michael J. Fox, Sean Connery, and even Lucille Ball. The town had a peaceful, welcoming vibe, and the thought of a hotel room, a shower, and a real bed was the ultimate luxury for a weary thru-hiker.

After checking into my hotel room, I brewed some fresh coffee in the small kitchenette and relaxed in front of the TV, soaking in the joy of simple comforts. A nap followed, and when I woke up, feeling refreshed, I unloaded my pack and headed into town for resupply. My empty backpack felt light as I wandered through the charming streets, heading to the grocery store to stock up on food for the next section of the trail. I had already planned my dinner for the evening—a big pot of spaghetti cooked in my kitchenette, a welcome break from trail food. The mountain air was crisp and clean, and I felt a strong camaraderie with every other dirty, tired thru-hiker I passed. We were all in this together, finding rest and recharge before hitting the trail again.

That evening, my spaghetti dinner turned out even better than I had imagined. With a full stomach and a deep sense of contentment, I fell into a peaceful, deep sleep. The soft bed was a far cry from my usual spot on the hard ground, and I woke the next morning feeling more rested than I had in weeks. After gathering my laundry, I headed to a local diner for a hearty breakfast—eggs, bacon, toast, and hot coffee. It was perfect fuel for what was shaping up to be a day filled with simple pleasures.

At the laundromat, I met other hikers. We sat around a picnic table outside, swapping stories of sore feet, dangerous climbs, and future indulgences. One topic dominated our conversation: the giant boulder we'd had to scramble over. But as much as we discussed the challenges, we also marveled at the beauty of the San Jacinto Mountains. And, of course, there was the shared excitement of all the unhealthy food we were planning to eat that day.

In the early days of planning my PCT adventure, I quickly learned from watching countless YouTube videos that reducing pack weight was a game changer. It starts with investing in ultra-light (UL) gear and extends to extreme measures, like drilling holes in your toothbrush handle to save a few grams. Many thru-hikers become obsessed with shaving off every ounce. On a scale of 1 to 5, where 5 is the most fanatical, I'd rate myself at a 2. I invested in some UL gear but did it on a budget, prioritizing comfort where possible. For example, I opted for a two-person tent over a single-person model. Although the larger tent added weight, I wanted the extra room for the 5 to 6 months I'd be on the trail.

When I arrived in Idyllwild, having already logged around 160 miles, I realized it was time for a "pack shake down" to get rid of unnecessary items. I laid out everything from my pack and sorted it into three piles: "must have," "trash," and "send forward." I threw out excess socks, underwear, playing cards, and unneeded medication. I also sent my ice axe and micro-spikes forward to Kennedy Meadows, where they'd be needed for the Sierra Nevada section, still 600 miles away. Additionally, I replaced my food bag with a lighter one, placing the old one in a hiker box—a communal place where hikers can leave items for others. After my shake down, I had shed about 5 pounds from my pack. While that might not sound like much, the difference it made while hiking 20 miles a day was immense. Before the trail, I thought my pack was already optimized, but after 160 miles, I realized I still had plenty of non-essentials. The trail teaches valuable lessons, and minimalism is among the most profound. The farther I hiked, the more I realized just how little I truly needed to survive.

This same principle applies to leadership. As a leader, it's essential to regularly conduct a metaphorical "pack shake down" in your life. Take stock of all the things you're carrying—whether it's family, work, hobbies, financial obligations, friendships, or other commitments. Many of us go through life adding more and more to our load, believing we can carry it all. What are we trying to prove, and to whom? Why do we feel the need to keep accumulating?

I used to live that way, too. After going through a painful divorce and filing for bankruptcy, I remember having a conversation with my pastor. He pointed out how burned out I had become, trying to do everything. That conversation was a wake-up call. I realized I had been carrying too much for too long. Many people don't realize they're living this way until a major life event forces them to stop and reevaluate. Why wait for that moment? Conduct regular "shake downs" and remove what's unnecessary.

In leadership, a well-balanced life is critical. If your life is cluttered with non-essential tasks or people who drain your energy, it will affect your ability to lead effectively. In your professional life, think about what might be adding unnecessary weight to your leadership. Perhaps you're holding on to underperformers who are dragging down the rest of your team, or maybe you've implemented redundant processes that create extra work without adding value.

I've worked with many leaders who, out of pride, create their own complex systems and spreadsheets, even when a perfectly adequate reporting system is already in place. In one of my restaurant management roles, I had three different Area Directors over five years, each with their own reporting methods. Learning a new system every time was time-consuming and frustrating. One Area Director stood out, though. Instead of adding layers of complexity, she implemented a "start and stop" list. We'd review what tasks to start and what to stop, focusing on what was critical to the business. Her minimalist approach allowed for streamlined, effective leadership and no wasted energy. She rapidly advanced in her career, likely in part because of her ability to keep things simple.

Many leaders get caught up in creating extra work to demonstrate their competence, but in reality, this often leads to long, unproductive meetings and burnout. Streamlining processes and focusing only on what truly matters leads to greater efficiency and success. As a leader, it's vital to conduct regular "shake downs" of your processes and systems. Don't let pride or habit prevent you from making adjustments and lightening your load. There's no need to wait until you're halfway through the journey, weighed down by excess baggage, to realize that trimming the fat would have made everything easier from the start.

CHAPTER 7

EMBRACE THE EVER-CHANGING TRAIL

After weeks of hiking through the arid, sun-scorched desert, it was both shocking and disorienting to suddenly find myself in a snow-packed section of trail, where the path ahead was almost impossible to discern. Navigating through the deep snow required me to rely heavily on my Guthook app, my lifeline for staying on track. But as luck would have it, I had recently lost my phone's charging cord, and with my battery down to just 20%, the situation quickly turned stressful. Every step I took was now weighed down by the growing anxiety of potentially losing my navigation tool. I found myself praying that I would come across another hiker who had a spare charging cord I could borrow, desperately hoping for a bit of trail magic to save the day.

Under normal circumstances, my hiking pace hovered around 2 to 3 mph. However, slogging through the heavy snow had reduced my speed to less than half that. At one point, I lost my bearings and had to backtrack about 2 miles to get back on the correct path. This mistake only compounded my frustration as my feet became drenched from the snow, leaving me cold and uncomfortable. Thankfully, as I made my way back, the trail became visible again. After several more hours of slow, exhausting progress, I finally stumbled upon a great campsite, complete with flat spots for tents, a large fire pit, and even a few picnic tables. It felt like an oasis after the long, challenging day.

As I began setting up camp, I was soon joined by a group of fellow hikers: Soul Sister, Tree Boy, Sweetness, and a few others whose names I can't quite recall. I had known Soul Sister since the very first day on the trail, but the rest were new faces to me. Tree Boy, an interesting character, was hiking the entire trail while carrying a small guitar with him. As we gathered around a crackling campfire for dinner, Tree Boy pulled out his guitar and played a few tunes while we shared stories about the day's hike. Despite the grueling conditions earlier, I felt a sense of joy and peace being surrounded by this group. It was one of those rare, precious moments where I felt truly content. There was no talk of jobs, money, or material possessions—none of the concerns of the outside world. We were just a group of dirty, stinky, tired, and hungry hikers, but most of all, we were happy, bonded by our shared experiences on the trail.

True to form, I woke up early the next morning before anyone else. I quietly packed my gear and set off around 4:00 a.m., the cold air biting at my exposed skin. I left camp fully dressed in my cold-weather gear, already nostalgic for the peaceful evening I had spent with the group. As the sun slowly rose, I began shedding layers, and by 9:30 a.m., I was hiking in nothing but shorts and a t-shirt. The dramatic temperature swings were no longer surprising to me. The PCT often took me from snow-covered mountains to scorching desert terrain in a matter of hours. I had come to accept that the trail was ever-changing and unpredictable, and I had to be prepared for anything it threw my way.

By the time I reached the bottom of the mountain, the wind had picked up, blowing fiercely at around 30 mph, with gusts that reached 45 mph. I was now back in the hot, dry desert, trudging through deep sand. Hiking in the sand was slow and grueling, with each step requiring much more effort than usual. The landscape had shifted to a barren, unwelcoming expanse with nothing but large, unattractive windmills looming on the horizon. The visual monotony, combined with the challenging terrain, made for a frustrating section of trail.

Eventually, I left the deep sand behind and found myself navigating a rocky section of the trail. Battling the wind and loose rocks, I was relieved when I finally stumbled upon a beautiful flat spot along the riverbank. It seemed like the perfect place to set up camp for the night. However, as I began pitching my tent, a sudden gust of wind caught it, and I watched in disbelief as it, along with my sleeping bag and pad, tumbled 100 feet into the nearby tree line. Setting up camp became a struggle against the elements, but after much effort, I eventually got everything secured. Once inside my tent, shielded from the relentless wind, I made dinner and reflected on the day's events. Writing in my journal, I started drawing parallels between the constant changes on the trail and the personal changes I had been experiencing in my life. The trail had an uncanny way of forcing me to confront thoughts and emotions I hadn't fully processed before.

As a leader, dealing with change is not just an essential skill—it's an art form. Not only do you have to navigate change yourself, but you also need to ensure that your team can handle it effectively. Entire leadership books are dedicated to managing change, highlighting its importance. My experiences on the PCT helped me realize that embracing the trail's constant shifts was crucial to survival. Fighting against the inevitable changes would only result in frustration and failure. I had no control over the wind, the terrain, or the weather. Instead, I focused on controlling what I could and adapting to the ever-changing environment.

In leadership, many people waste time and energy fighting changes they cannot control. Some leaders resist change so fiercely that they inadvertently create a culture of resistance within their teams, resulting in negativity and subpar performance. Knowing when to resist and when to embrace change is critical. A wise leader once advised me to "vent up the ladder, not down." This means if I disagreed with a change, I should voice my concerns to my superiors but never let my frustration trickle down to my team. If I didn't fully support a change, it would become infinitely harder to lead my team through it.

The key leadership lessons I learned on the PCT are that change is inevitable, and the only way to manage it effectively is to focus on what you can control rather than wasting energy resisting what you cannot. Although this chapter isn't a comprehensive guide to managing change, it serves as a reminder that change will happen. After discussing the change with your boss and accepting that it's going to occur, here are some steps to ensure the transition is smooth and minimally disruptive:

1. **Accept the Change**: Fully embrace the change and

focus your energy on controlling what you can, rather than dwelling on what you can't.

2. **Understand the "Why"**: There is often a valid reason behind the change. Understanding the rationale will help you guide your team forward more effectively.

3. **Communicate the Change**: Once you've accepted the change, communicate it to your team in a positive light. Avoid talking to your team if you haven't accepted the change yourself; your frustration will only hinder progress.

4. **Acknowledge Challenges**: Recognize and address any potential frustrations your team may have. Allowing open dialogue helps foster a more collaborative atmosphere.

5. **Seek Feedback**: Involve your team in the change process. Getting their input will empower them and foster buy-in, making the transition smoother.

6. **Implement the Change**: Once you and your team are aligned, implementing the change will be far easier and less stressful for everyone involved.

CHAPTER 8
NEVER "YELLOW-BLAZE"

In the world of long-distance hiking, "yellow-blazing" refers to the act of taking an unnecessary ride to skip ahead on the trail. While some hikers are compelled to bypass sections due to unavoidable circumstances like wildfires or other emergencies, taking shortcuts more than necessary is often seen as cheating and is highly frowned upon by the hiking community. I vividly recall enduring a particularly brutal stretch of the trail after leaving Aqua Dulce. This section was grueling, defined by intense heat, dryness, and a severe lack of water. I left Aqua Dulce around 8:00 a.m., having enjoyed a hearty breakfast at a local café. With a challenging 24-mile stretch ahead of me before the next water source, I set off carrying 5 liters of water and a full Gatorade.

The hike turned out to be excruciatingly difficult. Shade was an incredibly rare commodity, and whenever I stumbled upon even the smallest sliver of it, I would seize the opportunity for a much-needed break. The relentless heat was my primary concern, far surpassing any worries I had about encountering wildlife. Facing heat exhaustion or, worse, heat stroke in such a remote area, with no immediate help available, would have been truly perilous.

As I slogged through this brutal section, I came upon a highway where an opportunity for yellow-blazing presented itself. An old shuttle bus was parked on the side of the road, offering rides to a place called Hiker Town, about 25 miles ahead. Many hikers were opting for the shuttle because the trail ahead had been closed due to a wildfire from the previous year, which had made it too dangerous to hike. Our alternative was a "road-hike," essentially a hike around the burn zone on the highway. While the prospect of hiking 25 miles along a road was far less appealing than trail hiking, I chose to tackle the road hike rather than take the bus.

Watching the bus drive away, I plugged in my music and began the road hike. After about 5 miles, I arrived in a small town that had a café and general store. There, I ran into a fellow hiker named "Radio," whom I had encountered a few times on the trail. He insisted on buying me lunch, and I was more than happy to accept. I enjoyed a hearty BBQ sandwich with fries and a generous piece of apple pie topped with vanilla ice cream. Taking advantage of the café's restroom, I soaked my head under the sink faucet with cold water to cool off.

We spent about an hour and a half at the café, chatting about the upcoming stretch of the hike. When I left in the late afternoon, the sun was still scorching, and I headed toward an ostrich farm about 7 miles away. The bartender at the café suggested that I call the owner of the ostrich farm, who often allowed hikers to camp on her property. I arrived at the farm around 6:00 p.m. and found a decent spot to set up camp. To my pleasant surprise, I was the only hiker camping there that night. Exhausted from the heat, I was in no mood for conversation and just wanted to set up camp, do a little reading, and get some much-needed sleep.

The property had a reasonably good bathroom with cold running water. My feet felt like they were on fire from the heat radiating off the highway. The sink was too small and too high for me to wash my feet properly, so I decided to soak them in the toilet. While this might sound unappealing, my feet were far dirtier than the toilet, and the cold, swirling water felt amazing on my throbbing feet. I used some liquid hand soap to clean my face, neck, underarms, and other areas. I even managed to get my head under the faucet to wash my hair with the hand soap and then combed out the tangles. Despite my exhaustion, I found myself laughing at my unconventional situation—camping at an ostrich farm, bathing in a sink, washing my feet in a toilet, and loving every minute of it. The simplicity of it all was refreshing. Life on the PCT was brutally hard at times, but it was a "simple hard." There was no confusion, no complexity, just a life that made me appreciate even the smallest of luxuries.

As I reflect on this now, sitting here dressed for work and about to spend the next 10 hours making order out of chaos, I would gladly transport myself back to that ostrich farm in a heartbeat. The things I valued so much out there now seem almost meaningless in comparison. I can eat, shower, or rest whenever I want. Perhaps it's because we have so much stuff that we take these basic luxuries for granted. The joy I felt in cleaning myself at that ostrich farm is hard to explain to someone who hasn't experienced it. There was no chaos, no pressure, no unrealistic expectations—just me, the trail, and the occasional simple amenities that felt like pure luxury.

The next morning, I noticed that another hiker had set up camp at the farm. I wasn't exactly looking forward to the 14 miles of highway walking ahead of me. Highway hiking is incredibly monotonous, tough on the feet, and visually uninspiring. About 5 miles into the walk, I had a memorable encounter with my first rattlesnake—the first I had ever seen in the wild in my entire 51 years. The large rattler barely noticed me as I tried to get close enough to take a good video. It was preoccupied with a rat in its jaws and rattled only as if to say, "Leave me alone while I enjoy my breakfast."

The hiker from the ostrich farm eventually caught up with me while I was filming the snake. We chatted briefly and continued on. Not long after, a kind driver pulled over and handed us both ice-cold Gatorades. It was an incredibly refreshing and much-appreciated treat. We eventually reached Hiker Town that evening, which was bustling with hikers. Hiker Town isn't a real town but more like a small commune with about eight old wooden cottages designed to resemble an old hotel, general store, jail, or bar. It looked like a rundown Western movie set, but it was a cool place to camp for the night, complete with a community bathroom and shower.

As we sat around that evening, sharing hiker stories and enjoying our dinners, I felt a deep sense of satisfaction knowing I had chosen to endure the "road-hike" instead of taking the shuttle. There is a unique sense of accomplishment that comes from putting in the hard work to reach your destination. Despite the many challenges that lay ahead, the confidence I gained from this experience was incredibly encouraging.

The Pareto Principle, also known as the 80/20 rule, suggests that 20% of people shoulder 80% of the work. If you're part of that 20%, you understand the frustration of consistently doing your best while watching others slack off and make excuses for their lack of effort. This section is for those in that 20%. If you're not part of this group, you're simply a boss, not a leader, and there is a significant difference. Take pride in being part of this elite group and keep doing the right thing. Your hard work will eventually improve your environment, but it requires patience and perseverance.

There's a story that perfectly illustrates this principle. A young boy confided in his father about his struggles and desire to give up. In response, his father took him into the kitchen and filled three pots with water. In the first pot, he placed carrots; in the second, eggs; and in the third, coffee beans. After boiling them for 15 minutes, he asked the boy to feel the carrots, which had softened. Next, he asked him to break an egg, which had hardened. Finally, he asked him to sip the coffee, which had a rich aroma. The father explained that each item faced the same adversity—the boiling water—but reacted differently. The carrot became weak, the egg hardened, and the coffee beans changed the water. "Which are you?" he asked his son.

As a leader, how do you respond to adversity? Do you let your environment change you, or do you change your environment? Leading during easy times is one thing, but how you lead during difficult times is what truly defines you. Embrace the challenges and put in the hard work, even when it's tough. That kind of effort eventually changes the culture for the better, and it gives you a huge sense of satisfaction. Avoid taking shortcuts and stay true to your principles; it will not only strengthen your confidence but also prepare you for the larger challenges that lie ahead. I knew that if I took shortcuts or yellow-blazed early in the hike, I wouldn't be able to handle the bigger challenges that awaited me down the trail.

CHAPTER 9
ADVERSITY STRIKES

I awoke at 3:00 a.m., fully aware of the grueling 18 miles that lay ahead. The urgency to make it to town that day was palpable—my food supplies had dwindled to almost nothing. I was down to just two packs of oatmeal and a single protein bar. There was no option to split the 18 miles over two days; I needed to cover the distance in one push. On a normal day, 18 miles wouldn't seem insurmountable, but with the shin splints that had plagued me for days, it promised to be pure agony—roughly 47,000 painful steps. (Yes, I had painstakingly calculated that.) To this day, I'm still unsure if I was suffering from shin splints or anterior tibialis tendonitis (ATT), as some hikers with similar symptoms were diagnosed with the latter. Either way, the pain was intense, and every step was an ordeal. ATT or shin splints, it made no difference—the path ahead was going to hurt.

And this pain wasn't the only challenge I had been dealing with over the last 48 hours. My inflatable sleeping pad had also stopped holding air, leaving me to sleep on the cold, hard ground. I had been trying to make do by folding the deflated pad in half and cushioning it with extra clothing. I even put my backpack under my legs to give myself some slight elevation.

But no matter what I did, it was uncomfortable, and my sleep was restless. High winds had been my constant companion as well. The night before, they were so strong that one of my tent poles snapped, collapsing the tent on top of me. As I lay there, my mind raced to find a solution. I had no idea how I was going to set up my tent with a broken pole in these brutal conditions. That's when I remembered the tent pole splint that came with the tent—a 6-inch hollow metal tube that was designed for such emergencies. It fit perfectly over the break, and for a moment, I felt a small victory amid all the setbacks.

The wind, however, remained relentless. For days, it had battered me both physically and mentally. It blew nonstop, day and night, as if it had a vendetta against me. There was no reprieve. At one point, I found a massive boulder and crouched behind it, hoping it would shield me from the wind's unrelenting force. It provided some relief, but not the kind of indoor shelter I longed for. Later, I heard that some hikers behind me had it even worse, with the wind so fierce they had to crawl through a particularly dangerous section of the trail to avoid being blown off the ridge. As I hiked, it felt as if the wind was deliberately toying with me, pushing my pack hard, then suddenly letting up, almost causing me to stumble. It was as if I was locked in a battle with the trail itself, and at times, I questioned if I could keep going.

That night, after finally managing to set up my tent using the splint, I lay there feeling as though the trail was trying to break me. But upon reflection, I realized it wasn't trying to make me quit at all. The trail, much like a tough coach, was pushing me to my limits to show me what I was capable of.

It was giving me exactly what I had signed up for—a brutal mental and physical challenge. At 51 years old, the trail was reminding me that I still had plenty of fight left in me. In a way, it was rekindling a part of me that had been dulled by decades of routine and materialism. The struggles I faced on the trail were tough, but they were clear and simple. There was no confusion, no mixed messages, just me, the elements, and the will to keep going.

The following morning, the thought of getting out of my tent and facing the cold, dark, windy trail was unbearable. I dreaded it more than any morning I could remember. My legs ached, my body was sore, and mentally, I just wasn't ready. But I had no choice. I had to cover 18 miles to reach a point where I could hitchhike into town, and I knew it would be slow going due to my injury. By 3:30 a.m., I had packed up and started out. Miraculously, within minutes of hitting the trail, the wind completely stopped. I'm not one to claim divine intervention, but having just whispered a prayer for relief, it certainly felt like an answered plea. The stillness of the air was something I had taken for granted before, but now, it was a blessing beyond measure.

In addition to the calm wind, I experienced another unexpected reprieve—the excruciating pain in my shins subsided for the last four miles of the hike. It was as if my body knew I was nearing my limit and gave me a temporary pass to finish the day strong. When I finally reached the hitchhiking spot, I was able to catch a ride and made it to my hotel by 4:00 p.m. Exhausted but triumphant, I dropped my gear in my room and immediately headed to the pizza joint next door. I ordered a pizza, a large salad with ranch dressing, and a cold beer. That meal will forever stand out as one of the best I've ever had. Sitting there alone, filthy, sore, and ravenous, I was completely in the moment. The food, the cold drink, the satisfaction of having survived—it all felt like the greatest rewards life could offer. The challenges on the trail had been brutal, but none of them had caught me by surprise. I had anticipated hardships and had prepared myself mentally. There's something profoundly different about facing adversity that you expect versus the kind that blindsides you.

But adversity is not confined to the trail. It's a part of life—at work, at home, with our health, our finances, our relationships. As a leader, it's your job not only to manage your own struggles but also to help your team through theirs. Many leaders make the mistake of ignoring challenges, hoping they'll disappear on their own. I've learned that accepting the reality of a situation is the first step toward overcoming it. When I was 41, I found myself in the midst of a divorce after 19 years of marriage. On top of that, I had just declared bankruptcy after a business venture had failed. I remember standing outside the apartment complex I had moved into, wondering how everything had fallen apart so quickly. It felt like the life I had worked so hard to build was unraveling. But after some time, I realized that the only way forward was to accept my new reality, no matter how unfair it seemed. Wallowing in self-pity wouldn't help me or my kids, who were depending on me to lead them through this tough time.

I've seen many leaders in business refuse to accept the realities of a situation. Some think that acknowledging a problem is equivalent to admitting defeat. They ignore the facts, dismiss valid concerns, and demand harder work without addressing the root of the issue. I once worked for a company where food costs had spiked dramatically. During a meeting, one leader pointed out that prices from vendors had increased, but menu prices hadn't been adjusted to compensate. Instead of acknowledging the basic math, our boss dismissed the explanation and demanded a fix, telling us, "I don't want excuses; just fix the problem." It was as if he thought ignoring the reality would make it go away. But as leaders, how can we hope to find solutions if we don't first acknowledge the problem?

Facing adversity, whether on the trail or in life, requires honesty, resilience, and sometimes, solitude. The trail taught me that adversity, while painful, makes us stronger. As I sit here, reflecting on my own personal and professional challenges, I remember the words of a great leader who once told me, "There are two kinds of leaders: those who cower in the face of adversity and those who rise to meet it." The choice is ours. My advice—to both myself and you—is this: Acknowledge the adversity, find some quiet time to think, confront it head-on, and look forward to the stronger version of yourself that will emerge on the other side.

CHAPTER 10
ATTACK THE HILL

Hiking through the desert section of the Pacific Crest Trail (PCT) was an experience that pushed me to my absolute limits. At around mile 650, the conditions seemed to conspire against me in every possible way. I was losing weight at an alarming rate, often finding myself dangerously dehydrated despite my best efforts to stay hydrated. My shin splints had intensified to the point where every step was excruciating, and my feet were constantly sore from the relentless miles. To make matters worse, the high winds turned every step into a battle. Mentally, it felt as though the trail was deliberately throwing everything it had at me to force me to quit. It was as if the PCT was meticulously designed to test my endurance and resolve.

Imagine hiking 15 miles through the blistering desert heat, with no shade in sight, on a rugged trail strewn with large rocks. Every step felt like an ordeal, and the pain was relentless. Covering 18 to 22 miles each day amounted to approximately 57,000 painful steps, knowing that the next day would bring the same grueling challenge. Just when you think you're making progress, you're confronted with yet another long, steep climb. The frustration, anger, and demoralization were overwhelming, pushing me to the edge of my physical and mental limits.

It was during this brutal desert section that I developed a new mindset: "attack the hill!" Simply encouraging myself with phrases like "Come on, NightRanger, you got this" didn't seem sufficient anymore. I needed a more aggressive approach. Each climb became a battle, a contest of wills between me and the ascent. My determination was to defeat each climb as if it were my adversary, and I was resolute in my goal to emerge victorious.

The desert climbs were frequent and relentless, coming at me under harsh conditions. After struggling with many of these climbs and feeling like they were beating me down, I decided to shift my strategy. At the base of each climb, I took a brief break, drank some water, and pumped myself up with high-energy music from Kid Rock, White Snake, or Van Halen. My goal wasn't just to reach the summit; it was to conquer it with a triumphant mindset of, "Hell yes! I kicked that climb's butt!" The sense of accomplishment that followed was incredible. Despite the burning in my lungs and legs, the thrill of beating each climb was a rush. The adrenaline from such victories often carried me through the next several miles, sometimes all the way to my campsite.

Another tactic I found effective was to pop in a Jolly Rancher when I was about half a mile from the top of a climb. I discovered that a Jolly Rancher would last me for about that distance, providing a sweet burst of energy and flavor that made the final stretch of the climb much more enjoyable. Little indulgences like this had become precious luxuries on the trail, turning tough moments into more manageable and even enjoyable experiences.

When I first embarked on this adventure, my goal was to test myself both mentally and physically. By mile 650, I realized that I was facing more challenges than I had anticipated, but in a way, it was exactly what I needed. I began to tell myself, "You actually can do this." If I had managed to get through all this and reached a quarter of the way, why couldn't I continue for the rest of the journey? Something inside me was awakening, revealing that even at 51, I still had a lot of fight left. I was proving to myself that I wasn't finished yet and that I could live the life I wanted and be whoever I wanted to be.

Leading people is no less challenging. For those who have tried it, you understand how mentally and physically exhausting it can be. Often, you face intimidating situations that make you question your ability to handle the challenge. As a leader, you must accept these challenges head-on. There will be times when you feel overwhelmed—when your team is unmotivated, the work is tough, and expectations are high. It's in these moments that your leadership is truly tested. Anyone can lead when circumstances are favorable, but how do you lead when the going gets tough?

There are essentially two types of leaders in the face of adversity: those who are intimidated and allow it to defeat them, and those who confront adversity head-on. But confronting adversity requires more than just desire and willpower. It demands a process, a plan, and a strategy to complement your determination. Just as I had the drive and intensity to attack those climbs, I also followed a few basic steps to achieve my goal. I rested, drank water, and listened to music before tackling each climb. Similarly, in the business world, a leader's desire to succeed must be matched with solid planning and attention to detail.

From my experience in the restaurant industry, I saw many leaders with the desire to run a great shift but lacking a solid plan. They didn't always ensure they had the right number of people in the right positions, the correct amount of product, or the necessary supplies. Many leaders hoped for a successful shift without focusing on the fundamentals. Desire alone won't overcome poor planning and lack of attention to detail. The analogy is clear: alongside the drive to succeed, you must have a plan and follow through with the details.

Remember the goal I adopted when facing those tough climbs. Reaching the top wasn't enough on its own. I wanted to feel like I had conquered the climb. As a leader, you should approach overwhelming situations with that same attitude. Strive not just to overcome obstacles but to excel in facing them. The adrenaline and confidence gained from dominating a challenge will be a tremendous boost for you and your team. And when you're nearing the finish line, don't forget to reward yourself and your team with a little "Jolly Rancher" to help you finish strong.

CHAPTER 11
CELEBRATE MILESTONES

Hitchhiking into Kernville, CA, was an experience that tested my endurance and patience. By the time I reached this point, my shin splints had become a significant source of agony. After an exhausting 18-mile hike, I found myself walking down a hard, paved road, desperately hoping for a ride. My food supply was nearly depleted, with only a handful of sunflower seeds left, and my water was dwindling rapidly. With every step, the pain in my shins seemed to grow more intense.

As I trudged along the road, I tried to keep my spirits up, but the physical discomfort was overwhelming. My thoughts were focused on how desperately I needed help. Then, as if by a stroke of luck, a kind lady stopped and picked me up. She mentioned that she had noticed my stiff-legged, awkward gait and could see that I was in pain. Her concern was a relief in itself.

The 20-minute ride into Kernville felt like a lifeline. We chatted about the hike and various topics related to the area, which helped to distract me from my discomfort. The relief and gratitude I felt when she stopped for me were immense—almost as if I had won the lottery. After all, when you're exhausted, hungry, and eager to reach town, a ride is nothing short of a miracle.

Once she dropped me off at my hotel, I checked in, dropped off all my gear, and hobbled over to a local pizza place. I indulged in a much-needed meal, devouring an entire pizza. Afterward, I returned to my room, where I began the process of icing my shin splints. The next several hours were spent watching TV, treating blisters, and resting. Given the severity of my shin pain, I decided it was best to stay an extra day in Kernville to heal before returning to the trail. Kernville, a charming little "river town," had a lot to offer. The Kernville River flowed through the town, providing opportunities for rafting, camping, and fishing. I spent a couple of days enjoying good food, visiting a local church, and resting. By the time I was ready to head back to the trail, I felt rejuvenated, and my shins had improved by about 50%.

Returning to the trail after a break is always a challenge. You lose your "trail legs" after a period of rest and a change in routine. However, with my shin pain reduced, the first day back on the trail was manageable. I managed to cover about 12 miles with minimal pain, but as the day wore on, the discomfort surged back with full force. The last 5 miles of that day were particularly brutal. The temperature had soared to around 90 degrees, and my shins were throbbing. Reaching the campsite that evening was a struggle, but there were no closer campsites available.

When I finally arrived at the campsite, I was greeted by some fellow hikers I had met several miles back—Black Magic, LuLu, Sweetness, Tree Boy, and others. Tree Boy had made a lovely campfire, and we gathered around to eat dinner and share stories of our struggles. While I cherished the solitude of hiking alone, I also valued these moments of camaraderie with fellow hikers. It was comforting to hear that everyone faced similar challenges and that I wasn't alone in my struggles. I fondly remember those campfire gatherings, where a bunch of dirty, exhausted, and smelly hikers shared tales, cleaned up with wet wipes, and tended to blisters. It was a simple, yet profoundly satisfying experience.

The next morning, I woke up around 4:00 a.m. with a severe headache that made me feel nauseated. Even the slightest exertion, such as digging a cat hole, made my head pound. After finishing and burying my waste, I returned to my tent to rest. I managed to sleep until about 8:00 a.m., when Black Magic stopped by to check on me. He knew I usually left early, so he was concerned when he saw I hadn't yet started hiking. By around 9:00 a.m., I had shaken off the headache and felt well enough to pack up and start hiking again. Although I still felt a bit shaky, the hike that morning was incredible. The weather was perfect, and the trail was beautiful and easy.

That day, I had to cover about 16 miles to reach Kennedy Meadows. This milestone is significant for PCT thru-hikers, marking the transition from the desert section to the Sierra Nevada. Located at mile 702, Kennedy Meadows features a pleasant camping area, a small store, and an outdoor grill. It's slightly over a quarter of the way through the hike and is celebrated as a major milestone. I managed to cover about 10 miles before the shin pain returned. About 3 miles before Kennedy Meadows, I stumbled upon a beautiful area with a fantastic swimming hole surrounded by large, picturesque rocks. I took off my pack and shoes and spent about an hour soaking my shins in the cold water. This break provided some relief, but the last mile into Kennedy Meadows was still challenging.

Fortunately, during that final mile, I ran into Soul Sister. We hadn't seen each other for several hundred miles, and walking into Kennedy Meadows together was a delightful surprise. Her presence was a significant morale boost, helping me power through the last stretch. We had become good friends early on, and reconnecting at such a milestone was special. It's a memory I'll always cherish.

As you approach Kennedy Meadows, the general store's patio overlooks the trail where hikers arrive. As you walk up, everyone on the patio cheers for you, and the sense of community among thru-hikers becomes palpable. I spent the next five days at Kennedy Meadows, resting and icing my shins. I worried that five days might not be enough and that I might have to quit if my condition worsened. During those days, I mostly relaxed on the patio, elevating and icing my shins, eating at the grill, chatting with fellow hikers, reading, playing with the dogs, and getting to know the store's staff. It was a wonderfully relaxing five days that, thankfully, were just enough to fully heal my shins.

This journey taught me how important it is to stop and enjoy the adventure, instead of just grinding out miles. I kept reminding myself to stop and enjoy the experience. It took an injury for me to slow down and appreciate what I had accomplished. Leaders often face a similar situation. We can become so consumed with work and achieving goals that we forget to reflect on our progress and celebrate milestones with our teams. While my injury was personal, leaders impact not only themselves but their teams as well. If leaders continuously push forward without taking time to reflect and celebrate, they risk causing stress, frustration, low morale, and even high turnover.

I once had a tough boss named Sebastian, who was a relentless driver of results. He pushed himself and his team hard, but his leadership style had its merits. After several months of intense work, he would give us a break, inviting us to dinners, baseball games, or lunches. During these breaks, he would sincerely thank us for our hard work and achievements but focus on connecting with us personally rather than discussing work. His approach worked because he balanced relentless drive with well-timed breaks to celebrate our successes.

As leaders, we must remember to take breaks from our relentless drive and celebrate milestones. This approach not only boosts morale but is crucial for long-term success. Just as my long-term success on the PCT depended on caring for myself physically, mentally, and emotionally, long-term leadership success requires taking care of yourself and your team in the same way.

CHAPTER 12
MOUNTAINS vs HILLS

"Because in the end, you won't remember the time you spent working in an office or mowing the lawn. Climb that damn mountain!" – Jack Kerouac

Transitioning out of the desert section was so exciting! It's so funny how much you talk to yourself while hiking the PCT alone. I distinctly remember telling myself, "You're finally out of the desert"! I even remember talking to the desert, "Goodbye desert, I absolutely will not miss you"! I was rested, my shins felt great, and I was back! I felt great! I was rested, reinvigorated, and ready to tackle the next challenge, The Sierra Nevada section. I had talked to a lot of hikers about what we were about to transition into, and although it was exciting to be out of the desert section, we all knew that what was coming was going to be even more difficult. The hills we climbed in the hot, windy, dry desert section were only training us for what we were about to embark upon. In this transition from desert section to the Sierra Nevada section we were going to quickly go from an average elevation of about 5000 feet to an average elevation of over 10,000 feet. Although each section of the PCT has its own beauty, the Sierra Nevada section is well known as the most grandiose. This 390-mile section has a total elevation gain of 57,888 feet and passes through several national parks, such as Yosemite, Sequoia, and Kings Canyon. We would traverse seven different mountain passes ranging in elevation from 9,624 feet up to 13,153 feet at Forester Pass. There have been years when the Sierra section was closed off to hikers due to high snow fall. Fortunately for us, 2021 had been a relatively light snow fall year. While sitting at Kennedy Meadow and talking with other hikers, along with reading comments on the Guthook app posted by hikers ahead of us, we all decided that we would not need our micro-spikes or our ice ax. The snow and ice on the trail ahead of us was much less treacherous than in years past, so most of us mailed those items home to reduce our pack weight. Although we ended up replacing that weight with bear canisters that were mandatory in this section due to the large amount of Black Bears. Transitioning into a completely new hike was very exciting to me, and although there were a lot of conversations about the difficulty of this section, I felt very prepared.

Within 5 miles of hiking out of Kennedy Meadows the hike began to change. The water was quickly becoming more abundant, there were more trees, and some green grass. Walking along rivers with rushing water right next to me was such a refreshing experience. As I got further into this new section, I came across my first marmot sighting. Being from Oklahoma and Texas I had never even heard of a marmot before and had certainly never seen one. I was thoroughly enjoying this section and was taking more time to truly experience all it had to offer. Hiking in the perfect weather, with beautiful scenery, on a nice even trail was a true joy that I'll never forget. Now that we were in bear country we had to change our routine a little bit. Not only did we have to carry our food in a bulky bear canister, but we were highly encouraged to cook, and brush our teeth about 30 yards from our tent. We would also place our bear canister about 30 yards from our tent at night to ensure it didn't attract any bears. The goal was to keep as much scented stuff away from our tent as possible. We didn't want to do anything that might draw a bear to our tent.

It wasn't long before the ascent to 10,000 feet began. I remember noticing that once I started getting past 9,000 feet the elevation started having a physical effect on me. Breathing was more difficult, my pace had slowed down, and some slight headaches were coming on. Getting to my first camp site above 10,000 was exhausting. I was stopping about every half mile to catch my breath. My trekking poles had suddenly become very valuable to me. The trekking poles allowed me to use my arms to help with the steep climbs which took a little bit of the load off my legs. When I reached my campsite that evening, I was past exhaustion. Everything I did wore me out. I had to stop after every single task to catch my breath. Unload my pack, catch my breath; put in a tent stake, catch my breath; take off my shoes, catch my breath; and the most difficult task by far was blowing up my sleeping bad! Once I finally got my tent set up and made some dinner, I was too tired to eat. I would take a bite, then lie down; take another bite, lie down again. This continued for a about 30 minutes until I had finally finished eating. My normal nightly routine of brushing my teeth and giving my body a once over with a wet wipe took my last drop of energy. It was only about 6:00 p.m. and still very light outside, but I pulled my headband over my eyes and went straight into a coma.

Today is an exciting day! I finally reached my campsite at Crabtree Meadow where I would get a few hours of sleep before getting up at midnight to climb to the top of Mount Whitney. Mount Whitney is the highest peak in the contiguous United States at 14,505 feet and just a short detour off of the PCT trail. My plan was to set up camp, eat some dinner, get to sleep by 6:00 p.m., then wake up at midnight to try and make it to the peak by sunrise. Unfortunately getting to sleep didn't work out very well due to the large number of younger hikers in the campsite who decided to stay up a little later to smoke some weed and have some fun. I finally fell asleep around 10:00 p.m. which made the midnight wake up a little difficult. Once I was awake, had some coffee and oatmeal, and packed a very light pack (slack packing), I headed out in hopes of reaching the peak before sunrise. Since I would be returning to the campsite after summiting, I left my tent, sleeping system, and most of my gear at camp. My pack only consisted of some clothing layers, coffee, cooking equipment, snacks and water. Although I had only slept about 2 hours, walking off into the night with my headlamp lighting the way gave me all the excitement and energy I needed that morning. I knew that I was about to climb to a place that not many had been and not many would ever be able to go. After about 4 miles of this 7.5 mile climb I knew I was not going to make it by sunrise. My pace had slowed to about 1 mph due to the elevation and also because the trail had become very rocky and difficult. As I continued upward and the sun started shedding little bits of light on the mountain I was amazed at the beauty.

When you start your hike at night you get to enjoy the beauty of the night sky with all the stars, and then as that first light starts to come in you get to enjoy colors in the sky along with the beauty of the mountain. Its an experience that will force you stop and take in the beauty of God's creation. At about 13,800 feet I had began stopping about every half mile to rest for a minute and catch my breath. Fortunately we weren't dealing with any issues with snow on the trail since it was a light snow year, but we were seeing some patches of snow along the side of the mountain. By this point I had put on my puffy coat, gloves, and had my Buff covering my nose and mouth. The temperature had dropped a lot and the cold wind was brutal. The last mile of the trail was comprised completely of big rocks, some of which required some scrambling. Although I wasn't going to summit by sunrise I did happen to pass a window in the mountains that opened up perfectly to the sunrise and provided me with one of the best pictures of the entire adventure. Climbing up that final quarter mile section sore, tired, hungry, cold, out of breath, and just physically worn out I could see and hear the people ahead of me. What a great feeling when you know you've finally made it to the top. As I made me way to the summit area I was greeted with smiles, high fives, and great words of encouragement from people I had never even met before. It still amazes me at how quickly a bunch of strangers connected so quickly. There were no social classes or status symbols out here. Just a bunch of exhausted, dirty hikers who were all experiences the exact same challenges which made us all feel immediately like family. I made my way to a nice ledge to sit, drink some coffee, and just enjoy the amazing view from 14,505 feet, realizing that I may never climb to a point this high again in my life. While enjoying the view and reflecting on my recent journey, and life in general, I blessed to witness a fellow hiker kneel and propose to his girlfriend; she said yes!

Over the next several days we would climb up some very challenging mountain passes. Forester Pass at 13,200 feet, and Kearsarge Pass at 11,800 feet; shortly after summiting Mount Whitney at 14,500 feet had taken its toll on my body. These incredibly difficult passes were also teaching me some lessons about my previous mentality on attacking hills. It the desert section we did some challenging climbs and if you'll remember from one of the previous analogies, I had developed a mindset of aggressively attacking those hills. Just loading us some music, resting for second, then aggressively attacking that hill with the mindset that I was going to kick its ass. I learned quickly that climbing these passes was going to take a slightly different approach then just cranking up some tunes and aggressively attacking them. That approach worked great on those hills in the desert. But these mountain passes were much more challenging that those hills. These climbs were longer, steeper, and at a much higher altitude. I remember checking my heart rate occasionally on these climbs because I could feel my heart beating so hard and fast. I would be barely trudging along at about ½ mph, stop to check my heart rate and find that it was beating at about 140 bpm. If I took the exact same approach as I did on those desert climbs, I would have given myself a heart attack. Successfully negotiating these passes took patience, resting, and much more strategy. I started putting much more planning into these climbs. I would look at the details of the climb on our Guthook app to see where the climbs would level off a little. On all of the climbs there would be these very small sections where the climb would level off for about a ¼ of a mile before becoming steep again. I would make a note of these level sections so that I would know when I could take a small break. For me, knowing where the breaks were on these grueling climbs gave me some benchmarks to shoot for. It kind of broke it up for me in my head so that I didn't get as overwhelmed. This approach greatly improved my moral going into these difficult climbs. Knowing the details of the trail helped keep me from being caught off guard by any unexpected challenges.

Just like I had to have a different approach to these mountain passes verses the dessert hills, as leaders we also must have different leadership approaches depending on the situation and the variety of personalities that we are attempting to lead. I've always thought of leadership like a tool belt with a variety of tools that are used for various jobs. Your tool belt has a hammer, a chisel, pliers, a screw driver, and a wrench. Your job as a leader is to chose the correct tool based on the situation, the personality, the task, and the goal. I've worked with leaders who seem to only have one tool in their tool belt and they use that in every situation with every person with only sporadic success. Had I not altered my strategy on navigating these difficult mountain passes I would have never made it. I would have either injured myself or just burned myself out and quit.

When the task becomes more difficult we have to change our approach. There could be a variety of reasons why the task has become more difficult. It could be that the project is just more complex, or it could be that you have a new team on the project who has less experience. Whatever the reason is that the task has become more difficult is irrelevant, the point is that as a leader you must assess the situation accurately and ensure that you leadership style fits the current circumstances.

Driving myself up those smaller desert climbs with an aggressive attacking mentality worked great in those circumstances. Using that same aggressive attacking mentality in the Sierra Nevada section would have been disastrous. Just like if you as a leader take an aggressive attacking mentality in the wrong situation will prove to be disastrous.

As the difficulty level of the climbs quickly increased I found myself relying heavily on my trekking poles to take some of the strain off my legs. Those long, steep climbs with a 30lb pack on your back set your legs on fire quickly. You quickly learn that you have two other limbs that can greatly contribute to the climb by adding in all those muscles in your arms, shoulders, and back. Why solely rely on your legs muscles when you have other resources that can help shoulder the load. Adapting your leadership to more difficult challenges should include utilizing all your resources to shoulder the load. The people you work with will always be your greatest resource. You have bosses, support staff, and subordinates who are all willing to help. It may take a little "pride swallowing" on your part, but reaching out to your team for help is vital in certain situations.

Learning to assess the upcoming difficult climb to find the steepest sections, the "level off" breaks, and the distance greatly improved my moral. Before I learned to do this, I would go into these climbs with no vision, not knowing how far I had to go, were the breaks were, or how steep it was. I would get so frustrated and angry when the climb suddenly got steeper, after a small level section it would suddenly go right back up again, or if it just seemed like the climb would never end. Leaders must provide the vision for their team. We need to assess the task and ensure we know how hard it will be, how long it will take, what resources we'll need, and where the benchmarks are along the way that will allow us to catch our breath and celebrate our progress. Providing our team with no vision will lead to extreme frustration, low morale, poor productivity, and high turnover. There are plenty of times as a leader that taking the attacking aggressive approach is very necessary and beneficial, it's just important to remember that each situation and set of circumstances may require a different approach.

CHAPTER 13
ALTERNATE TRAILS

The John Muir pass is a "must do" for any hiker. The morning that I headed up the 7-mile climb that would take me from an elevation of 9,000 ft to over 12,000 ft was beautiful. I hiked through some of the most beautiful country in the world. Walking along side rushing water with gorgeous waterfalls, surrounded by big green pine trees and engulfed by huge mountains painted white with snow all around me was something that I just wanted to absorb into my soul so that I would never forget this experience. We had a light rain the night before so to add to the beauty I was seeing with my eyes, I was blessed with the freshest smell of rain that I had ever experienced. Not even the tremendous number of mosquitos that swarmed around me could ruin this experience, although they gave it their best shot.

I needed to move quickly today because I needed to get 18 miles in to ensure that I was able to get into the town of Bridgeport by Wednesday. I had a planned "zero day" in Bridgeport where I would re-supply on food, go to the post office to get the Father's Day present that my kids sent me, and rest in a hotel that I had already reserved. I had made the reservation several miles back when we had an internet signal, but since we would not have a signal before the exit point to hitch into Bridgeport, I would not be able to change that reservation. I was a little too aggressive with my timeline to get into Bridgeport which meant that I was really going to have to hump it to make it on time.

By the time I made it to the top of the John Muir pass and rested for a bit in the famous John Muir cabin I knew I was in trouble with my plan to get into Bridgeport by Wednesday. The climb down from this pass was painfully slow. As I was getting closer to the bottom, I was stopped by a park ranger who was randomly checking for PCT permits. I was talking to him about my Bridgeport timeline trouble and he turned me onto an alternate trail that ventures off the PCT and would get me into Bridgeport about 8h -12hours faster. Since this alternate trail wasn't on our Guthook app, I jotted down the directions he gave me and decided to give it a shot.

The next day I came to this alternate trail location and decided to go ahead and give it a shot. The trail had obviously not been traveled in a long time. The path was very grown over with grass and weeds, but it was still recognizable. As I started making my way up the pass in the humid 85-degree weather I stopped for a quick water break and noticed the first signs of a storm coming in. I was being conservative with my water because I had no idea when I would come across another water source. Abandoning the Guthook app map meant that I had to completely wing it for a while. I would not know where water was, how long the pass was, where campsites were, or what kind of elevation gains I would encounter. For the last 800 miles I had become very accustomed to knowing exactly what to expect during each segment. There was a slight feeling of insecurity building that would only grow stronger as the journey progressed. The storm that I noticed earlier was coming in and bringing some rain with it. This was the first time in over 800 miles that I decided to break out my rain jacket. By the time I had reached, what I thought was the top, Summit Lake at 10,203 feet the temperature had dropped to about 65 degrees and the storm looked to be getting stronger. There was thunder and lightning coming from exactly where I was heading. I passed a couple doing some hiking and camping at Summit Lake. They were coming from the opposite direction and let me know that I was heading into some strong storm conditions. It did give me a small sense of security to see some hikers up here, at least I knew that I wasn't completely out in the middle of nowhere. As I continued along the trail, I just kept going up higher. By this point I really thought I would be climbing down which was really starting to concern me. At about 11,300 feet I found myself very isolated in some cold, windy, rainy conditions climbing up a trail that was comprised completely of large gray flat rocks. I stopped to make a quick video of this situation because I didn't want to forget how it felt to feel lost and a little panicked. It was starting to get dark, and I wasn't 100% positive where I was. I didn't know how much further to the trail head, how much more elevation I had to climb, or if there were any decent campsites coming up. All I knew was that a park ranger told me that this pass would get me to where I wanted to go, approximately how many miles the trail was, the elevation of the trailhead, and that I was on the exact path that he told me to take. Those were the only reassuring thoughts that I had to keep from going into full on panic mode. Eventually the trail did lead me over the mountain and to the descent on the other side. As I crossed over the mountain and started heading down, the wind picked up to the point that it started pushing me down the mountain. The strong wind and cold rain were brutal by this point. I found a small cluster of trees that gave me some slight shelter from the wind where I unloaded my pack to get my puffy coat, gloves, and beanie out. I had now gone from 85-degree weather with shorts and a t-shirt, to about 35 degree weather with a coat, beanie, and gloves. My shoes and socks were soaked with the cold rain which made my feet feel like they were frozen. Tired, worried, hungry, cold, and unsure of how much longer I had to go I continued slopping through the wet trail until out of the corner of my eye I caught a glimpse of a trailer. I can't explain to you the happiness and relief I felt when I saw that trailer. Seeing that trailer meant that there was a campsite, and a campsite most likely meant that the trail head was close by. Before I started hiking this trail, I did a little reading on-line about it. I had taken a screenshot of the article that happen to mention that the trailhead was at 9600 feet. My Garmin In-Reach showed that I was currently at 9800 feet, which meant that I was only a couple hundred feet from the correct elevation. Therefore, if I stayed on the trail for just a little longer, surely it would take me right to the trail. Just as suspected, I walked right to the trailhead! The relief and the sense of accomplishment were hard to put into words! By the time I found a good camping spot, and got my tent set up I was freezing. I quickly got out of my wet clothes, put on some dry clothes, and zipped myself up in my sleeping bag. I was simply too exhausted to cook any kind of dinner, so I just lay there in my sleeping bag trying to warm up, ate a few bites of peanut butter, and passed out sound asleep. The next morning, I packed up all my gear and headed to the trailhead. At the trail head there was a little general store that had a small restaurant attached. I sat there at the counter drinking hot coffee and gorging myself on pancakes and bacon. I had survived one of the most challenging experiences of my life and sitting here having breakfast at this very moment was truly one of the most satisfying experiences of my life.

Is it ever OK to take a risk and "venture off the map" as a leader? If so, how do you know when it's the right time to take that risk? It is my belief that as a leader you will inevitably find yourself in many situations that will require you to decide if you should take some risk and "venture off the map". When making this decision its important to look at the "risk vs reward". In the situation I was in on the trail, the reward was worth the risk. Getting into town 8-12 hours faster was a huge reward considering how badly I needed to re-supply on food and I didn't want to miss out on my hotel stay. I desperately needed to rest, clean my gear, clean myself, and re-supply on food. When a leader is contemplating taking some risk it's imperative to ensure that the reward is worth the risk. There must be a solid potential reward and a necessity for considering the risk. Calculating the level of risk is another key component. If you are going to take the risk, you need to do your due diligence to calculate the level of risk. Are the odds in your favor that you'll succeed? In my situation I had a trusted source that suggested the alternate trail, I clearly found the trail sign pointing me in the correct direction, I had a decent idea of the mileage, I knew the elevation of the trailhead, and I knew there would be water at some point. As I was approaching the alternate trail and found myself getting concerned about the risk of going off the map, I would calm myself by relying on these things. I knew the reward was worth it, and I new the risk had a high probability of success. Success wasn't guaranteed, but the odds were in my favor. As a leader in the business world, you must do your due diligence to mitigate the chances of failure. Talk to other leaders, research the data, and get some feedback from your team. Knowing that you have put some serious research into your decision will greatly help you stay motivated when things get difficult, and you start having doubts. I remember when I was standing in the windy, cold, rainy weather at 11,300 ft feeling like I may have made a bad decision. Even though I felt a small amount of panic setting in, I still felt 75% sure that I was going the right way which helped me get past the panic and keep trudging forward. When you make the decision to take some risk, and you find yourself feeling a little panicked that you may have made a bad decision; just stop for a minute and remember the due diligence that you put into making this decision, then regain your composure and press on.

CHAPTER 14
TRY SOME NEW SHOES

I never expected hitting the 1,000 mile mark to be met with some slight depression. By this point I'd seen so much beauty, gotten past so many obstacles, met some amazing people, and started actually feeling like an adventurer. Yet, instead of feeling extreme excitement and joy, I was experiencing my first feelings of depression. This journey is just such a grind! Day in and day out you're tired, sore, dirty, and hungry. It's so easy to get caught up into just grinding out miles that you very often forget to enjoy the journey. That's a very good analogy for our journey through life. We often get so caught up in trying to power through the daily grind that we forget to enjoy the journey. Hitting that 1,000 mile mark and realizing that I still wasn't even half way yet was just a little overwhelming at that moment. I had allowed myself to think too much about how much further I had to go to finish and had to reel my thoughts back in and focus on those short term goals.

The trail had transformed to hotter, dryer conditions. We were descending out of the Sierra Nevada section and getting into the Northern California section which was known to be hotter and dryer. I remember loving how the trees looked in this area. Giant trees with green lichen covering them. Being from Oklahoma and Texas, lichen is something I had never seen before, and I was amazed at how beautiful it was. The slight depression I felt earlier didn't last long as I started to regain some appreciation for the beauty of the trail. Because of the easier terrain my daily mileage had been getting back into the 22-25 mile range. We were no longer climbing over those long arduous passes that made getting in a 15 mile day very difficult. Battling through the rocky terrain of the Sierra section, not to mention having hiked over 1,000 miles, had really wreaked havoc on my feet. By the end of the day I would be left hobbling the last 5 miles praying that the campsite I was hiking to would suddenly just appear. I had just accepted that incredibly sore feet was just part of the experience and that there was nothing I could do about.

As I arrived in South Lake Tahoe for a much needed zero day to rest, re-supply, and clean up I stopped into a local hiking gear store. They had a huge selection of trail runners, and since I had over 500 miles on my current shoes, I decided to buy a new pair. I was planning to stick with the same brand I had used for the first 1,000 miles. I had watched a lot of videos and read a lot of articles about the best trail runner to wear on this hike. The Altra Lone Peak was well known as the best shoe to wear on this trail. I had trusted all these sources and worn it for the entire journey up to this point. Changing shoes at this point in the hike was highly discouraged by most sources. The owner of the store, who happened to have some training in podiatry, encouraged me to abandon the Atra's and go with the Hoka Speedgoat. He said that Atra's were great for some people but felt that my foot shape was much more suitable for the Hokas. I tried them on and was amazed at how stable and comfortable they'd felt! I couldn't believe I'd went over 1,000 in the Atra's when I could have been in the Hokas the entire time. Walking the 2 miles from the gear store to my hotel was a pleasure in these new shoes. I had a new sense of excitement that maybe I'd found something to make the journey less painful, and more enjoyable. While walking to my hotel I walked right past Lake Tahoe. A beautiful blue lake surrounded by big snowcapped mountains. There were people riding jet ski's, boating, and just lying on the sandy beach. Walking past the lake watching all these people out enjoying themselves made me wish I could spend an extra day here, rent a jet ski, and just take a break from hiking. My personality has always been the type to keep moving forward until the job is complete. Stopping to take an unplanned break was not my nature. But then I remembered how I was trying to change some things about my nature. One of the things I wanted to change about myself was to stop overthinking things and just act of some impulses. So I added another night to my hotel stay and spent a day out on the lake jet skiing. Even something as enjoyable as hiking can take it's toll on you mentally, especially when it's as long and difficult as this hike is. Taking an extra day to just relax, enjoy life, and break up the monotony was amazing. Riding that jet ski around the lake, taking in the scenery, and just enjoying the sun and the water gave me a massive moral boost. On these zero days we always end up walking several miles around town to find a laundry mat to wash our clothes, find a place to go eat, and to find a store to re-supply on food. As I was walking to the hotel I noticed people cruising around on these electric scooters. I had never ridden an electric scooter before, but I said, "what the heck", rented a scooter and rode all over that part of town I thoroughly enjoyed my time in Lake Tahoe.

Back on the trail I found myself hiking much faster than before and had no foot pain. There was a dramatic difference with these new shoes. I felt kind of like an idiot for waiting this long to switch shoes. I look back now and think I may have even been able to avoid the shin splints had I started with these Hoka's. I had been over 1,000 miles with continuous foot pain and stuck with the same shoes because that's what everyone suggested. I had just come to accept that hiking with extreme foot pain was unavoidable and just part of the experience. Had I not met that store owner who encouraged me to try a new shoe, I probably would have just continued with the same shoe and possibly ended up with enough pain (or injury) to end my journey.

By mile 1115 my spirits were high. We had crossed our final mountain pass and we were walking through some beautiful country. Tall green tree's, smooth trails, and beautiful weather. Northern California was experiencing a heat wave at the time but up here in the mountains the weather usually didn't get above 75 degrees. I was finished with the Sierra Nevada section and was now entering the Northern California section of the PCT. Of the 5 sections of the PCT, Northern California was number 3 and would finish out the state of California. If felt like we'd been hiking through California for a year and the thought of finally being able to cross into a new state was very motivating. My confidence was growing stronger every day, and with the new shoes I felt like I was flying through the miles. You don't really appreciate being pain free until you've had to go through miles and miles of pain.

Too often as leaders we're afraid to try something new. Even when what we're doing is causing us pain, we sometimes just continue to stick with it. It's not always that we're necessarily afraid to change something, sometimes its just that we don't even consider making a change. The thought of changing something never even enters our minds. Even when deep down in our souls we know that something isn't working, too often we just ignore it and accept that this is just the way it is. I would strongly encourage you as a leader to be brave enough to ask yourself the question, "is this how it has to be"? Is there something about your leadership style that needs to change? I know we've all heard the quote from Albert Einstein, "Insanity: doing the same thing over and over again and expecting different results". I don't think that leaders consider this quote often enough. I am certainly not advocating for going into an organization and just changing multiple things just for the sake of change. I'm speaking more about doing some serious self-reflection and considering changing something about your leadership style. Maybe it's how you're leading one specific individual that isn't working, or maybe it's how you're leading the entire group. But when you notice the pain, and the pain just continues to get worse, you must at the very least ask yourself if something else may work better. I hiked for over 1,000 miles with pain before I decided to make a change. Why? Why did it take me so long to change shoes? Was it because all my research told me that those were the best shoes? Was it because everything I read highly suggested not switching shoes in the middle of long thru hike? Was my pride getting in the way of accepting that I may have been wrong in my original shoe choice? Was I afraid that the pain would only get worse if I switched? The answer to all these questions is "yes". All these things had contributed to my belief that hiking with this foot pain was just the reality of this journey. Had I not met the owner of the shoe store who evaluated my foot and steered me to a different shoe, I would most likely have just stuck with the same shoe. Fortunately I met him before it was too late, made the switch, and drastically improved the comfort of my journey. I am by no means insinuating that you need to abandon your entire leadership philosophy, your character, or your morals. My point is that during your leadership journey there will often be times when it will be necessary to back up, self-reflect, and decide if there is a subtle change that will help improve the comfort of the journey for you and your team. Years ago, as a much younger leader, I was opening a new restaurant as the General Manager. I had three very experienced managers and one manager with very little management experience. I, along with the three experience managers, marched into this journey with "guns blazing". We were all so busy and working so hard that we didn't notice that Sean, the less experienced manager, was getting left behind. My Director of Operations mentioned to me that she didn't think Sean was going to make it. She said he didn't really seem to care, and that we needed to consider moving on without him. I asked her to please allow me a little more time to work with him before we gave up on him. This was the first time, as a young leader, that I recall thinking to myself that I needed to adjust my leadership style. I had three other managers who had a lot of experience, knew their stuff well, and were just as

CHAPTER 15
MANAGING WILDFIRES

Navigating around wildfires on the Pacific Crest Trail (PCT) has become an accepted reality over the years. It's been several seasons since anyone has been able to hike the entire PCT without dealing with closures caused by wildfires. Hikers often have to resort to "road-walks" or hitchhiking to get around these closed sections. I had planned a stop in Quincy, California, to re-supply on food, rest, and pick up a package that a friend had sent me. At that point, I didn't even realize a wildfire was near until the person who picked me up asked, "Are you getting off the trail because of the fire?"

Little did I know that park rangers were already evacuating hikers due to the wildfire that had flared up in the area. The "Dixie Fire" was raging across the region in 2021, and by the time it was all over, it had burned more than 960,000 acres, becoming the second-largest wildfire in California's history. It even completely destroyed the nearby town of Greenville.

Once I reached my hotel, showered, unpacked my gear, and took a nap, it seemed like the fire had exploded in size. Standing outside, staring at the huge plume of smoke accented by an ominous red sky, I felt fear creeping in. I feared that the PCTA (Pacific Crest Trail Association) would close the entire

Northern California section of the trail—about 500 miles. Worse, I feared that I might unwittingly put myself in danger by venturing back onto the trail.

The next day, I spent my time resting, eating, and glued to the news. I was determined to gather as much information about the fire as possible, but none of it was promising. I learned that not only was the Dixie Fire raging, but there were also massive wildfires burning up north in Oregon. I had anticipated missing a few small sections of the trail due to fires, but the thought of missing several hundred miles was deeply discouraging.

When I went into town to resupply on food, I encountered more hikers than I had seen in the previous 1,200 miles combined. Many were being forced off the trail from several miles back, as the fire had grown immensely. I spoke with several hikers and eavesdropped on many conversations about how to handle the situation. Some hikers were extremely frustrated, some were genuinely frightened, and others seemed almost indifferent. I landed somewhere in the middle.

I had made a promise to my kids before the journey began: I would be cautious and avoid doing anything foolish. I had already broken that promise a few times on this trek and didn't want to push my luck by venturing into another dangerous situation. In those conversations, I noticed about 75% of the talk was complaints. Many hikers were upset about missing parts of the trail, frustrated that they wouldn't be able to say they walked every single step of it, or disappointed that they would miss some of the scenic landmarks they had looked forward to. Their frustration made sense, and I got why they needed to vent.

However, one group of hikers was reacting in an extreme manner—yelling, cussing, throwing their gear, and even kicking their packs. I felt bad for them, knowing full well where their anger came from. Each of us had overcome enormous adversity to get to this point. We had seen hikers drop out due to injuries, exhaustion, sickness, personal issues back home, or even depression. Tragically, we had also heard of two hikers who lost their lives back in the desert section.

Yet, here we were, still standing and still enduring the journey. And now we were being forced off the trail by something entirely out of our control. That realization—"out of our control"—was key for me. Sure, I allowed myself a few minutes to vent, but after that, I focused on the next step. I couldn't do anything about the wildfire; my task was to figure out the safest way to continue. Expending valuable mental and physical energy on complaints wasn't going to help; I needed to conserve that energy for the path ahead.

Ultimately, several other hikers and I decided that taking the bus to Chester, skipping around 40 miles of trail, was the most reasonable option. Others chose to play it safer and took the bus further, to Burney, missing about 125 miles of trail to put themselves well ahead of the fire.

Waiting at the bus stop with about 50 other hikers was quite a sight. Some of us had managed to snag a hotel room and clean up, but many weren't as lucky. Regardless, we all looked like a gaggle of dirty hobos sprawled out on the sidewalk at the small bus stop in Quincy, California. Once we boarded the bus, it was packed to the brim—hikers were crammed in like sardines.

The temperature was around 80 degrees that day, and the heat only enhanced the pungent aroma of dirty hikers. But by that point, none of us cared. We had all grown used to the smell, almost seeing it as a badge of honor. Despite everything, the mood on the bus was surprisingly upbeat. It seemed like everyone had finally accepted the reality of the situation. We talked about the next section of the trail, shared excitement about finishing California, and even cheered loudly when someone on the bus announced that we had just passed the halfway point of the PCT. Sure, it wasn't the celebration we had envisioned for reaching mile 1,325, but we celebrated nonetheless.

When we arrived in Chester, an eerie feeling hung in the air. As we walked from the bus stop to the grocery store, everyone seemed mesmerized by the falling ash and the thick cloud of smoke hovering over the town. Despite the unsettling atmosphere, we managed to hitch a ride from Chester to the trailhead at Lassen National Forest. We walked into the light smoke, bandanas tied around our faces, hoping they would protect us from breathing in too much smoke.

The next morning was strange, a surreal mix of smoke and fog as I made my way through the dark, quiet forest. The trail eventually led to a clearing just as the sun began to rise over the mountains. I just stood there, looking at the sun painted a deep, blood-red hue from the blanket of smoke resting over the land. In all my years, I had never seen anything quite like it.

Accepting the reality of our situation with the wildfires, and focusing on what we could control, were crucial elements in continuing the journey. Over the years, I've encountered many people in leadership roles who refuse to accept reality.

Some seem to believe that acknowledging a challenging situation is the same as making excuses. I couldn't disagree more. How can you overcome an obstacle if you refuse to recognize it?

On the flip side, I've also seen leaders who acknowledge an obstacle but use it as an excuse to fail rather than as a stepping stone toward a solution. When I hear a leader shut down any discussion of an obstacle with phrases like, "I don't want to hear excuses," I immediately think that leader lacks wisdom—and, frankly, the ability to acknowledge reality. This dismissive attitude comes across as mentally lazy, a way to push the problem onto subordinates because they don't want to deal with it themselves.

For example, if a general manager tells their Director of Operations they are struggling with sales growth because a competitor has opened across the street, and the director shuts them down with "I don't want to hear excuses," that's not leadership. It's avoiding the reality of the situation because they either have no solution or are too lazy to address it.

Similarly, when a general manager lists every reason their business is failing without mentioning a plan to overcome those obstacles, I recognize a leader lacking maturity and the mental toughness necessary to lead. Just like with the wildfires we faced on the trail, you must first acknowledge the reality of the situation. Then, formulate a plan to overcome it by focusing on what you can control. Don't waste valuable energy on what you can't control. Instead, acknowledge the obstacles and start strategizing how to move forward, based on the elements within your control.

CHAPTER 16
PERFECTLY TIMED "TRAIL MAGIC"

Hiking through Lassen National Forest and Lassen Volcanic National Park stirred up memories of the desert section of the PCT. It was a hot, dry stretch with barely any water, reminding me of the extreme challenges that define parts of this trail. If you've seen the movie *Wild*, this is the area where Cheryl Strayed, played by Reese Witherspoon, made the critical mistake of not packing enough water for the 100-degree heat and came dangerously close to severe dehydration and heatstroke. Before venturing into the infamous Hat Creek Rim section, I came across a camping area equipped with some picnic tables and water spigots. It was around 11:00 a.m., and the temperature was rising quickly. I set my pack down and found a shady spot on the picnic table to eat lunch and hydrate. Just as I was preparing to hit the trail again, two hikers joined me. Their trail names were "Wake and Bake" (due to his morning ritual of smoking weed) and "Tattoo." We talked about the upcoming brutal heat and the lack of water in the next section. They were planning to stop for the day and rest at the campsite, attacking the Hat Creek

Rim early the next morning—a strategy that sounded tempting.

As we chatted, they asked if I wanted some "fungus." At first, I had no clue what they meant until they explained that the "fungus" was psychedelic mushrooms, commonly known as "shrooms" or "magic mushrooms." They claimed it made the hike far more enjoyable. While the offer was intriguing, I felt that with the challenging conditions ahead, it was better to have all my senses fully engaged.

After about seven miles of hiking through the heat, I took a break in a shaded area, noticing that my body was covered in a fine layer of black dust. Leaning against a tree, I laughed at how filthy I had become. My hands, dry and cracked from the sun, were lined with dirt, giving them the appearance of someone much older. Making it through the 26-mile, waterless stretch of Hat Creek Rim was a feat in itself. As I passed through a burn zone left behind by last year's wildfires, the scorched landscape resembled something out of a post-apocalyptic film. I could feel my motivation waning. I was hot, sore, tired, and incredibly thirsty. I still had about 10 miles to go to my campsite when, out of nowhere, I spotted a sight that felt like salvation: an ice chest nestled under the only shade tree I'd seen for miles.

Cautiously optimistic, I walked up to it, praying it wasn't empty. When I opened the lid to find a fully stocked chest with fresh ice, sodas, chocolate milk, and water, I felt like I had just won the lottery. Of all the "trail magic" moments I had experienced on the PCT, this was by far the most perfectly timed. I set down my pack, grabbed an ice-cold ginger ale, and took a much-needed break. As I sipped my soda, trying to cool off, a female hiker strolled up, dressed in a skimpy tank top and—of all things—a G-string. You encounter a wide variety of characters on the PCT, but this was a first for me. We chatted for a bit, and as she walked away, I chuckled to myself—not out of judgment, but more out of amusement at how there really are no rules out here. Everyone hikes their own hike and does whatever it takes to make it to the next campsite without collapsing.

It was a bit comical seeing someone hike in a G-string, especially considering that every visible (and likely not visible) part of her body was coated in dust and dirt. But sitting there, under that tiny sliver of shade, sipping an ice-cold soda, and getting some unexpected entertainment was just what I needed. It gave me the boost of energy and motivation to power through the last 10 miles of that grueling hike.

Those final 10 miles were far from easy. The heat was relentless, the landscape offered little to no shade, and my body was exhausted. But my mood had shifted dramatically. That simple act of "trail magic"—a cooler stocked with drinks—had lifted my spirits and provided the mental reset I needed to keep going.

Looking back on it, a small reward at the right moment can have a huge impact on morale. Whether on the trail or in the workplace, people often need these little gestures of appreciation to push through tough times. Leaders, in particular, can take a lesson from this. Far too many overthink the concept of rewarding their teams, believing it requires some grand, elaborate gesture. In reality, it's often the simplest of rewards—a spontaneous acknowledgment, a small gift, even a kind word—that can make all the difference. Unfortunately, some leaders don't believe in rewarding their teams at all. They think the paycheck is reward enough and that employees should be grateful to even have a job. I strongly disagree.

Leaders who are truly engaged with their teams can sense when morale is dipping and know when a little boost is needed. It doesn't take much, but it requires paying attention. When I think back on all the "trail magic" moments during my hike, I can distinctly remember how much each one lifted my spirits during the most challenging stretches. Trail magic didn't happen often, but when it did, it was incredibly timely and deeply appreciated. So, why wouldn't a leader want to take the time to reward their team occasionally? High morale leads to happier people, and happy people are almost always more productive.

The parallels between the PCT and leadership are undeniable. Just like a small act of kindness from a stranger can reignite a hiker's determination, a leader's thoughtful recognition of their team's hard work can revitalize a workforce. The key is in understanding that it's not about the size or expense of the reward—it's about the timing, sincerity, and acknowledgment of effort. Sometimes, all it takes is a cold drink in the middle of a desert.

CHAPTER 17
REMOVE THE PEBBLE

Burney, California, a small mountain town in Shasta County with a population of about 3,200, is located around mile 1,420 on the PCT. I had planned a zero day in Burney to resupply food, pick up a package from the post office, clean up, and get some rest. Not more than five minutes after getting out of my hitch, I ran into an old hiking friend, Soul Sister. We hadn't seen each other for several hundred miles—maybe not since Kennedy Meadows back at mile 700 on the PCT. I bumped into her right outside the local gear store, where I had stopped to pick up some new socks.

We were both excited to reconnect and sat outside the store, catching up on how our hikes had been going. We talked about how disappointing it was that many of the views had been obstructed by wildfire smoke. After chatting for a few minutes, we parted ways again. I had just arrived in Burney, and she was on her way back to the trail.

After spending two nights in town doing all my typical "town chores," I left my hotel, ready to get back on the trail. But before heading out, I stopped at a local diner to enjoy a big breakfast. As I was finishing up, the waitress mentioned that we were close to Brighton Bridge, the bridge from the famous 1986 film *Stand by Me*. In that iconic scene, the boys are running across the bridge, trying to outrun an approaching train. I've always loved that movie, and after a bit of research, I found that it would be a very small detour from the PCT. I didn't usually take spontaneous detours, but this time, I decided to make it a short hiking day and check out Brighton Bridge.

The hike to my campsite was about seven miles, followed by a six-mile out-and-back trek to the bridge. By this point in my journey, a 13-mile day felt like a relaxing stroll. Once I reached my campsite, I set up my tent, sleeping pad, and sleeping bag, along with the rest of my gear. I wanted to make sure that when I returned from the bridge, everything would be ready for me to settle in. I also wanted to travel light to the bridge, so I only packed some water and a snack.

While resting at my campsite, I had taken off my shoes and socks to give my feet a break. When I got set to head to the bridge, I accidentally left my gaiters behind. For those unfamiliar, gaiters are light pieces of material that cover your ankles and clip onto your shoes. They're designed to keep rocks, sand, and other debris out of your shoes, which helps prevent blisters. Since the bridge was only a six-mile round trip, I figured I wouldn't need the gaiters and pressed on.

Not even half a mile into the hike, I felt a small pebble in my shoe. At first, I tried to ignore it, shaking my foot to shift the pebble to a less annoying spot. But as I continued walking, the pebble kept creeping back to an uncomfortable position. I found myself focusing more on the pebble than the beautiful scenery. Rather than stopping to remove it, I kept walking. Eventually, the pebble settled right next to the ball of my big toe. I tried to shake it loose, but it wasn't budging. I did my best to ignore it, thinking, "I've dealt with way more pain over the last 1,400 miles. There's no way I'm letting a tiny pebble force me to stop now."

When I finally reached Brighton Bridge, I was disappointed to see a blockade preventing access. I later learned that a man from Reno had died a few months earlier after jumping off the bridge, which led to its closure. With a bit of resourcefulness, I found a way around the blockade and walked across the bridge, snapping some memorable pictures.

The hike back to my campsite turned out to be more challenging than I had expected. The day had gotten pretty hot, and I hadn't brought enough water. As I trekked along the three miles back, I found myself wishing for someone to stop and offer me a ride. At least the heat and thirst took my mind off the pebble in my shoe. As I started daydreaming about an ice-cold soda, I stumbled across a small general store in McArthur-Burney Falls Memorial State Park. I hadn't even realized this park was nearby, let alone that I was within walking distance of a store.

I treated myself to an ice-cold ginger ale and an ice cream sandwich, then sat outside the store, watching local hikers enjoy their day. While I was there, I finally took off my shoe and removed the annoying pebble that had been bothering me for miles. It had rubbed a hot spot on the ball of my big toe, which I hoped wouldn't turn into a blister. I found myself wishing I had just stopped and removed it when I first noticed it.

The last half-mile back to my campsite was incredible. My belly was full of junk food, the pebble was gone, and I got to stop and take in what many people say is the most beautiful waterfall in all of California. I couldn't believe I hadn't known about Burney Falls before, but I was so glad I'd happened upon it.

The leadership lesson here is pretty clear: the pebble in the shoe is like that team member who damages the culture you, as a leader, are trying to establish. Just as the pebble was irritating, painful, and distracting to me, disruptive team members can have a similar impact on your organization. Over time, they cause lasting damage, much like the blister the pebble created on my foot.

The first step in preventing these "pebbles" from harming your culture is to ensure they never make it into your organization in the first place. If I had put my gaiters on, I wouldn't have had to deal with the pebble at all. In your organization, your hiring and training practices are your "gaiters." By establishing solid hiring and training procedures, you can avoid the discomfort and pain that come with having the wrong team members.

Great Hiring Practices: Your First Line of Defense

Conducting thorough interviews, solid reference checks, and detailed background checks significantly reduce the chances of letting a "pebble" slip in. During interviews, pay attention to more than just the answers to your questions. Observe if they smile, put thought into their responses, make eye contact, and show enthusiasm. While their answers are important, these additional cues are equally telling.

To properly assess these qualities, you must be a great listener. That means you need to *shut up* and let them speak. The 80/20 rule applies here: the interviewee should do 80%

of the talking, while the interviewer should only do 20%. Unfortunately, this rule often gets flipped. I've seen leaders dominate the conversation during interviews, making it impossible to gauge if the candidate is a good fit.

Even with excellent hiring practices, there's no guarantee a pebble won't sneak in. This is where a great training program comes into play. A robust training period allows you and your team to identify potential pebbles early on, reducing the risk of long-term damage. Yes, it's frustrating to invest in training only to let someone go, but it's far less costly than allowing them to stay and disrupt the team over time.

Why didn't I stop and take off my shoe to get rid of the pebble as soon as I felt it? Maybe laziness played a part, but more often, it's the belief that we can shift the pebble around to a less painful spot. Leaders do something similar with bad team members: they think they can move them to a different role where they might be less disruptive.

While moving people around can be an excellent practice for team members who fit your culture but aren't thriving in their current role, it's not a solution for pebbles. When you've identified a true "pebble," don't waste time trying to find a place for them. Instead, politely show them the door.

The key is determining whether someone is truly a "pebble" or just a team member in the wrong role. This doesn't have to be overly complicated. Some clear indicators include being argumentative, consistently late, lacking integrity, making excuses, being pessimistic, and acting selfishly. When these traits become apparent, don't hesitate. Get that pebble out of your organization.

As a leader, you owe it to your entire team to address the pebble quickly. Always remember to put on your "gaiters"—your solid hiring and training practices—so that you don't have to deal with the pebble in the first place. But if a pebble does sneak into your shoe and you've confirmed it's a true pebble, stop, take off your shoe, and dump it out. You already have enough on your plate as a leader; you don't need the added stress of a pebble rubbing a blister on your organization.

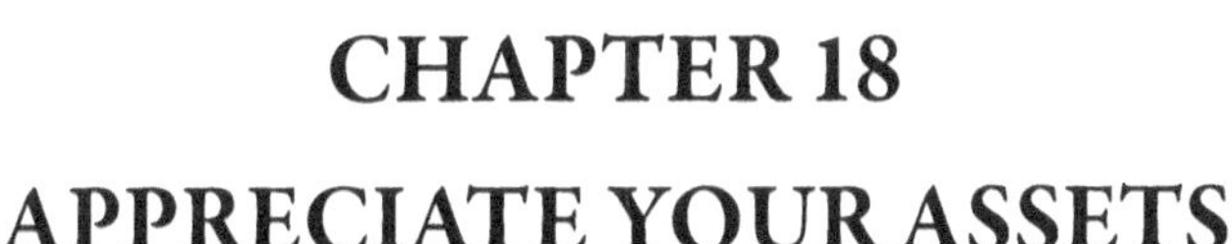

CHAPTER 18
APPRECIATE YOUR ASSETS

"The only way to deal with an unfree world is to become so absolutely free that your very existence is an act of rebellion" –
Albert Camus

Crossing into Oregon was one of the most exciting moments of the entire journey! California had been beautiful, diverse, challenging, and undoubtedly a life-changing experience. However, stepping into a new state felt like an enormous milestone, offering a strong sense of accomplishment. We had spent so much time and covered so many miles through the varying landscapes of California that entering Oregon finally made it feel as though we could glimpse the light at the end of the tunnel. By the time we crossed into Oregon at around mile 1700, we felt like veteran hikers. We had trudged through arid deserts, climbed to elevations exceeding 13,000 feet, navigated around wildfires, endured injuries, faced water shortages, braved treacherous winds, and hiked almost 2,000 miles! Our legs were solid, our lungs operating at full strength, and we were leaner and fitter than ever.

That said, crossing into Oregon wasn't quite the experience I had imagined. After surviving the heat of Northern

California, I had envisioned Oregon as a cool, lush, tree-covered paradise. However, Oregon was in the midst of an unusually intense heatwave, and instead of relief, we faced more blistering temperatures. Still, despite the unexpected heat, the excitement of finally entering a new state remained strong.

One day stands out vividly. The heat was oppressive, and the trail was littered with downed trees from a fierce storm that had passed through the year before. The reports said about 400 trees had been blown over, many of which had fallen directly onto the trail. It was both fascinating and eerie to see these enormous trees, snapped like toothpicks, lying across our path. Navigating through this maze of blowdowns was no easy feat. Often, it wasn't just one tree across the trail, but several tangled together, with thick branches that created massive obstacles. I remember more than once having to throw my pack over the trees, then crawl underneath, flat on my stomach, trying to wriggle through without getting snagged on the jagged branches.

I marveled at how well my pack held up during all of this. That pack became like a trusted companion. To anyone who hasn't hiked long distances, it might sound odd, but thru-hikers will understand this bond. The pack, along with my tent, sleeping bag, and water filter, were my lifelines—the only things I could count on day in and day out. Of course, there were moments of frustration. I recall a time when my pack developed an annoying squeak in the shoulder straps. No matter how many times I adjusted it, the sound persisted, driving me mad. Once, in a fit of frustration, I threw it to the ground, fuming over the noise. But despite these minor annoyances, the pack never let me down. It survived the heat, the rain, the dirt, and every bit of punishment I put it through, remaining steadfast. Today, it sits in my garage, waiting for another adventure. It may not be able to survive another 2,000-mile trek, but I will never part with it. It was my constant, reliable companion through the most adventurous five months of my life.

After finally navigating the maze of downed trees, I stopped for a break and checked the Guthook app for information on the upcoming miles. Some hikers had mentioned an alternate trail leading to Ramona Falls, which they described as an unmissable detour. On their recommendation, I decided to take the alternate route, and I'm so glad I did. The trail quickly descended into a dense, shaded forest, and the temperature dropped by about 10 degrees almost instantly. It was a welcome relief after the heat and strenuous hiking. As I approached Ramona Falls, I was greeted by one of the most breathtaking sights I'd ever seen. The waterfall cascaded over a cliff, framed by bright green trees and plants, with an old wooden log bridge crossing just in front of it. The whole scene felt like something out of a movie. I stood on the log bridge for a while, letting the cool mist from the waterfall wash over me, trying to soak in the moment. I knew that this, like all moments, would soon fade into memory, and I wanted to hold on to it just a little longer.

This experience made me reflect on how crucial my pack and gear were to my survival. Even when certain pieces of gear frustrated me or began to wear down, I knew that taking care of them and making necessary repairs was key to my success. As a leader, we must recognize that the assets under our control are critical to achieving our goals. However, no asset is more important than our people. A General Manager might survey their restaurant and see ovens, grills, tables, chairs, computers, and refrigerators as vital to the operation. A good GM understands the importance of maintaining these assets, investing time and money into their upkeep to avoid costly repairs. But a truly great leader knows that their people are their most valuable asset.

A great leader knows their success is completely tied to their team. Just like my gear on the trail needed care, people need development, support, and sometimes a bit of "repair" too. Leaders who value their team invest in them—training, coaching, counseling, discipline, rewards, and appreciation. People are at the center of any successful operation, and what they can do far exceeds what any piece of equipment can do. Your people can make your success or sink it faster than any broken machine ever will.

So, why do so many leaders fail to grasp this fundamental concept? Why do they so often place more value on physical assets than on their people? I've seen leaders who are quick to fire someone for underperformance, believing the next person they hire will somehow be better. However, hiring is always a gamble. No matter how great someone seems in an interview, you never truly know what you're getting until they're on the job. These leaders may end up regretting that they didn't take the time to develop the person they let go.

I once took over a restaurant that had a turnover rate of 320%. To put that in perspective, restaurant turnover is notoriously high, usually around 120%. So a turnover rate of 320% was an indicator of severe leadership problems. Despite the disastrous results, the existing management team was deeply resistant to change. They clung to their old ways, refusing to acknowledge that their leadership style was failing. In my view, this reluctance stemmed from arrogance. They were too proud to admit that their approach wasn't working.

In all the leadership books I've read, I've never once seen arrogance listed as a positive leadership trait. On the contrary, humility is frequently cited as one of the most vital qualities of a successful leader. Humble leaders understand that they need their people in order to succeed. They know that their team is the key to long-term, sustainable success. While you might achieve some short-term gains with a top-down, authoritarian style, the journey becomes far more arduous, and success less enduring, in the long run.

Treating your people as your greatest asset isn't complicated. Any seminar on employee retention will tell you the same basic principles: provide people with the tools they need to succeed, create fair schedules, show appreciation, respect diversity, build relationships, and invest in their development. These actions will come naturally when you truly value your people. When you reach that moment of understanding—when it clicks inside you that without your team, you will fail—you'll begin to see that your people are your most important asset. When that shift happens, your leadership will evolve, and your path to success will become infinitely more attainable.

CHAPTER 19
HIKING FAST

As we were approaching Crater Lake, we all knew that we were getting close to the campground that had a general store and a restaurant. It was going to be a 26-mile day in very hot weather, but we were determined to reach the campground before everything closed for the day. The day was full of arduous, boring hiking through miles of burnt landscape due to the previous year's wildfires that had ravaged the area. There were no opportunities to stop at beautiful spots to take in the scenery. It was all just charred, ugly trees. Despite how challenging the hike was that day, we maintained a fast pace. Not only were we hiking quickly, but everything we did that day was fast. Filtering water, bathroom breaks, and meals were all done with speed. By this point in our journey, these tasks had become instinctive, second nature. We didn't have to think anymore, which allowed us to do everything much faster.

Even though our bodies had adjusted to walking long distances by now, the last few miles that day were exhausting. I remember arriving at the campsite with aching shoulders, legs, and feet. I was in so much pain that I nearly lost my appetite for real food at the restaurant. Still, I made it back to the camping area, set up my tent, and hobbled over to the restaurant. Sitting on the patio, eating pizza, French fries, and drinking gallons of soda with my friends, I felt a sense of pride. I had become adept at this whole PCT journey. Every day was still mentally and physically difficult, but I had become skilled at all aspects of it, and that gave me a deep sense of satisfaction. My confidence in completing the hike was sky-high at this point. I knew that, barring any unforeseen accident, I could handle any obstacle between there and the Canadian border. It was a great feeling.

That feeling of accomplishment only grew the next day when I sat on a ledge overlooking Crater Lake. I don't think my writing skills can adequately describe what it felt like to sit and take in that perfect view. It was a sunny, 65-degree day as I sat there, trying to soak up every ounce of that view. I wanted to absorb it into my soul so that I would never forget the peace and happiness I felt at that moment. With a depth of 1,943 feet, Crater Lake is the deepest lake in the United States and the seventh-deepest in the world. Its captivating blue water, a result of its clarity and depth, is breathtaking. It's a view that stays with you forever. I sat there for about an hour, writing in my journal, thinking, and thanking God for giving me the opportunity to experience this incredible moment.

Listening to a high-level college football coach talk about "playing fast" reminded me of this experience. He emphasized the importance of his players practicing fundamentals and running plays so often that they became habits. He wanted everything to be instinctive for them so they wouldn't be slowed down by thinking. For them to "play fast," they needed to react based on instinct and muscle memory. If they had to think about every action, they would always be playing slower than needed to be champions. It was all about repetition—doing the same things repeatedly until it became ingrained in their DNA.

As I listened to him speak, I thought about some of the work environments I've been in. The restaurant I'm currently leading has only been open for about 60 days. That means everyone on our 80-person team is still very new. We have no "veterans" to rely on. The entire team is learning, growing, and gradually becoming better at their jobs. They are still making mistakes and learning from them, slowly learning to "play fast," but they're not there yet. As leaders, we must balance challenging them while also being patient. If we were to rush increased profitability by reducing staff to boost short-term gains, we would ultimately hurt long-term profitability.

Leaders must be in tune with their teams' abilities to know when to push them harder. The only way to stay in tune with your team is to be in the trenches with them, working, talking, and coaching alongside them. A great leader doesn't just stand on the sidelines yelling for the team to "do better." A great leader fights alongside their team. Leading this way allows you to know your team intimately, understand their capabilities, and gauge how hard you can push them. Pushing your team too hard, too fast, will only result in dissatisfied customers and frustrated employees. Allowing your team the time to become proficient at their jobs leads to happier employees, lower turnover, increased productivity, and a loyal customer base. All of this builds a strong foundation for long-term profitability.

As the leader of your organization, resist the temptation to prioritize short-term profits by squeezing too much out of your team too soon. Doing so will lead to the almost inescapable cycle of frustrated employees, high turnover, and poor customer loyalty. Believe me, that is not a cycle you want to be stuck in. Give your team the necessary time to learn how to "hike fast" before you push them into a difficult section of the trail that they aren't prepared for.

CHAPTER 20

THE COMMON PATH ISN'T ALWAYS THE BEST PATH

As I wrote about earlier, Oregon was much warmer than I had expected, and certain sections were much less abundant in water than I had anticipated. I had just come through a fairly hot, dry stretch when I arrived at a beautiful rushing river surrounded by large, flat stones—perfect for taking a much-needed break. I always loved finding spots like this, where everything seemed to align perfectly for a lunch break. I found an ideal spot right by the water, unloaded my pack, and gave myself a quick wash in the cold river. The crisp, cold water was incredibly refreshing on my dirty, overheated body, and I felt revived almost immediately.

Once I was cleaned up, I grabbed my water filter and began filtering some water. I was down to half a liter by this point, so I needed to filter about three liters—enough to get me through lunch and carry me to the next water source. There's nothing quite like fresh, clear, cold river water after it's been filtered. No bottled water in the world can compare to the taste of that pure mountain water. Honestly, the water likely didn't even need to be filtered, but none of us were willing to take any chances with something like Giardia. A bout of Giardia in the wilderness could easily derail your entire journey and potentially end your hike. As I sat there filtering water and soaking in the moment, I sat there thinking about how precious these simple, perfect moments were.

During times like this, when everything seemed to be in balance, I often found myself reflecting on the nature of time. It's a strange thing—no matter how hard you try to hold onto a moment, to soak in every detail, it eventually slips into memory. I was acutely aware that my time on the PCT was finite, that soon I would be back in the "real world," away from these beautiful, quiet moments. While part of me was eager to finish, another part of me knew that one day I'd look back and long to be right here, in these perfect moments by a rushing river, enjoying the simplicity of the trail.

After finishing my break, stretching out, and hoisting that heavy pack back onto my shoulders, I continued down the trail. It wasn't long before I encountered a strong-flowing river that I needed to cross in order to continue. River crossings weren't uncommon on the PCT, but they always required caution. This particular river wasn't deep or especially dangerous, but it was fast enough that I knew I had to be careful. The risk wasn't so much about drowning, but more about the possibility of slipping on a rock, twisting an ankle, or even breaking a leg. Minor injuries in the wilderness can turn into major problems quickly, especially when you're deep in the backcountry, far from medical help.

As I stood at the edge of the river, surveying the situation, I decided to search for a safer crossing than the one directly in front of me. The trail had led me to this particular spot, but it didn't seem like the best option. As I walked along the riverbank, scanning for a safer way across, I noticed a few other hikers also searching for their own crossings. There were a few places I considered, but based on the force of the river and the spacing of the rocks, I decided to walk a little further upstream to see if I could find a better option.

Eventually, I came to a section where a combination of rocks and fallen tree trunks provided a potential crossing. A fellow hiker was already on the other side, and it appeared he had crossed here, so I decided to give it a try. Slowly, I stepped onto the first rock, carefully testing its stability and slipperiness. Using my trekking poles for balance, I moved from one rock to the next with deliberate caution. The log I had to cross next was a bit trickier. It wasn't wide enough to plant my trekking poles on either side for balance, so I had to rely on my own sense of equilibrium, which is no small feat with a 30-pound pack on your back.

Although I wasn't in danger of drowning if I fell, being about three feet above the fast-moving water with sharp rocks below made falling a very unappealing prospect. The possibility of injury felt very real. I stepped cautiously, one foot in front of the other, testing each step to ensure I had solid traction and that the log was stable. It took only about five steps to reach a much safer area, but those five steps felt like an eternity. Once I was safely across, I turned and watched as three other hikers used the same crossing, and then I continued on the trail.

Whether you're leading a team at work, your family, or even a youth sports team, you'll often find yourself walking down the common, well-trodden path. In many cases, if not most, that common path will be the best and safest option. But as leaders, it's important to take the time to at least consider that there may be a better way, especially when faced with a difficult or challenging decision. Sometimes, walking along the edge of the river and considering alternate routes can lead to better outcomes. A path that's never been tried might turn out to be the best choice.

That day by the river, I seriously considered every option—even crossing at the trail's original point. I wasn't trying to be different for the sake of it; I was simply seeking the safest and best route. As a leader, the same caution must be applied when deciding to take a different path. A leader who chooses to go a different route solely for the sake of being unique is being arrogant and selfish. Only when the common path doesn't appear to be a good option should a leader seriously consider forging a new one.

The common path is common for a reason. It's been tried, tested, and proven to be safe for many before you, and it will likely be a safe option for you and your team as well. My point is that while it's essential to have the vision and courage to explore new paths, it's equally important to have the humility to stay on the common path when it's the best option. As a leader, you're responsible not only for your own success but also for the success of your team. This responsibility is not something to take lightly. When considering a different path, make sure you've done your due diligence and kept pride out of the equation. Leadership requires a careful balance between having the courage to forge a new path and the wisdom to recognize when the common path is best for everyone.

CHAPTER 21
TRAIL EVOLUTION

"*A mind that is stretched by a new experience can never go back to its original dimension.*" —Oliver Wendell Holmes

I can't even begin to count the number of times I reflected on how the trail seemed to be in a constant state of flux. When I say "the trail," I'm not just talking about the physical path we were walking on. I'm referring to the entire experience of the trail—the changing landscapes, the shifting weather, the fluctuating elevations, the variability in water sources, the ever-present bugs, and all the different camping spots. Every element contributed to the dynamic life of the trail. Change was an intrinsic part of the experience, and if a hiker didn't embrace this fact early on, they were unlikely to make it to the end of their journey.

Earlier, I described how it sometimes felt like a battle between me and the trail. It seemed as though the trail was doing everything in its power to prevent me from finishing, while I was doing everything I could to complete it. Constant change was one of the trail's most effective tools for challenging hikers. As I neared the end of the Oregon section, I encountered three new hikers who were heading into Cascade

Locks, Oregon, at the same time as me. Cascade Locks is a charming little town right next to the Columbia River and conveniently close to the PCT. It's where travelers cross the iconic "Bridge of the Gods" from Oregon into Washington.

There was a real joy in walking into Cascade Locks with these new friends, knowing we were about to enjoy a great breakfast before embarking on the final stretch of the PCT. Reflecting on this moment, I can't help but feel a pang of nostalgia for the person I was just a short two years ago. I had traveled 2,200 miles through diverse and challenging conditions, experiencing a freedom that few people ever get to enjoy. It was a freedom from the daily grind and from caring about others' opinions. We walked into town looking like dirty hobos, but we couldn't have been happier. The joy we felt was a unique kind of elation that only comes from a true sense of freedom.

Just inside the town limits, we stumbled upon a fruit stand. The woman running the stand cheerfully announced, "Free peaches for all PCT hikers!" Free food was an offer too good to pass up. I vividly remember her warmth and friendliness as she handed us the peaches. I'm not exaggerating when I say that I've never tasted fruit so delightful. Standing on the edge of the Columbia River, taking in the stunning view of Washington and the majestic "Bridge of the Gods," we ate those peaches in silence. It was a moment filled with mixed emotions: the joy of being in that beautiful place and the bittersweet realization that we were entering the final stretch of our journey. After finishing our peaches, we exchanged glances and headed to a local restaurant for breakfast.

At the restaurant, we dropped our packs outside and found a table by the window with an incredible view of the bridge. I ordered my usual—pancakes, bacon, and coffee—and took the opportunity to charge my electronics. By this point, charging devices had become as routine as going to the bathroom. As we enjoyed our breakfast and chatted as if we'd known each other for years, it was clear how quickly we'd bonded despite having only met a few hours earlier. I genuinely miss the connections I made on the PCT. After breakfast, I bid farewell to my new friends, stopped by a small grocery store to restock my food supplies, and headed back to the trail. While my new hiking companions planned to stay in Cascade Locks for a couple of days to rest and clean up, my plan was to push on into Washington.

Walking across the "Bridge of the Gods" felt surreal. It marked the transition into the final phase of the PCT—Washington. With only about 450 miles remaining, the significance of crossing this bridge was profound. I knew that it was unlikely I would ever undertake such a journey again, which made this moment even more meaningful. There's probably an analogy buried in that experience somewhere, but its significance was palpable.

That day, the hike was unusually hot. The morning had been cold enough to warrant my coat, but by now, I was down to a t-shirt and shorts. No more than a mile into the Washington section, I began hearing a strange creaking noise. I would stop, look around, but never saw anything out of the ordinary. As I continued through the heavily wooded trail, the noise persisted. After about ten miles, I arrived at a campsite near a clean creek. The sun was setting, and the temperature was dropping. By the time I had set up camp, filtered water, and prepared dinner, I was back in my coat.

That night, the strange creaking noise continued, waking me about ten times. I thought I had heard every conceivable nighttime noise by this point, but this one was baffling and a bit unsettling. I couldn't figure out what could be making such a sound just inside Washington that I hadn't heard throughout the entire journey. It wasn't until I was about two miles into my hike the next morning that I realized the noise was coming from the tall trees swaying in the wind. I'm not sure why the tall trees just across the river in Oregon didn't make the same noise, but even after 2,200 miles, the trail was still throwing me a curveball. The trail was stunning that morning—the sun was out, the temperature was perfect, and the greenery was lush and green.

As I approached lunchtime, I began looking for a great spot to rest, enjoy a break, and eat one of the peaches I had bought at the fruit stand. A light drizzle started to fall. Since I had rarely encountered rain over the previous 2,300 miles, I wasn't too concerned. Eventually, I found a lovely spot under a large tree that provided some shelter from the drizzle. As I had lunch and relished the juicy peach, the temperature dropped about ten degrees, and the rain intensified. I decided to put on my rain jacket, pants, and rain cover for my pack. It felt like the trail was giving me a preview of the changes it had in store for me. But by this point, I considered myself a seasoned "thru-hiker," ready for whatever new challenges the trail might present.

Change is an inevitable part of life. It impacts marriage, parenting, work, health, spiritual journeys, and every other aspect of our existence. Instead of trying to escape it, it's better to embrace and manage it. Change often gets a bad rap, largely because it's mismanaged. I believe that mismanagement stems primarily from two issues: creating unnecessary change and poor communication regarding the change.

When a leader is considering making a change, they need to ask themselves several crucial questions: Why is this change necessary? How will it affect the team, both positively and negatively? Is this the right time for the change? Leaders often make unnecessary changes due to boredom or ego, implementing alterations simply to "stamp their mark" or to do things their way. When a leader steps into a new role and starts making changes without understanding the existing team, it can be perceived as a slight. It might seem as though the leader is saying, "What you were doing was wrong; now we're doing it my way." Teams often work hard to achieve success, and a new leader's changes can feel like an unwelcome critique.

It's essential for leaders to thoroughly assess whether a change is genuinely necessary. Once a change is deemed necessary, the next crucial step is effective communication. This involves meeting with the team, explaining the rationale behind the change, acknowledging potential challenges, and soliciting feedback. I've found it useful to ask the team to "shoot holes" in the idea—essentially, to identify potential problems without focusing on positives. This approach not only provides valuable feedback but also helps gain buy-in from the team. When the team feels they have been part of the process and their voices have been heard, implementing the change becomes significantly easier. Without buy-in, leaders might face resistance and difficulties during the implementation phase.

I recall a time when, as an Area Director with responsibility for five restaurants, I wanted to change how our host teams managed a particular aspect of their job. I consulted with my General Managers and hourly host team members to gather feedback. After listening to their input, I decided against implementing the change. The host team raised valid points about why the idea wouldn't work well. This experience highlighted the importance of seeking input from all levels of the hierarchy. Leaders should avoid arrogance and be open to feedback from any available source.

When promoting a new General Manager, I would require them to refrain from making any changes for the first 90 days unless they consulted with me first. While this might seem like micromanagement, it underscored the importance of managing change effectively. I wanted to understand their reasoning and be involved in the communication process with their team. After working together for 90 days, I felt confident that the new leader was well-prepared to manage change moving forward. The key takeaway is that while change is inevitable and often necessary, it must be motivated by genuine need and managed with a well-thought-out process.

CHAPTER 22
INITIATE THE SLIDE

Hiking through snow in late August was a wild and unusual experience for someone from Texas. In Texas, outdoor activities are usually confined to the early morning hours to avoid the sweltering 100+ degree temperatures that can persist throughout the day. In contrast, I found myself in the refreshing chill of the Cascades, surrounded by the stunning peaks of Mt. Adams, Mt. St. Helens, and Mt. Rainier. The snow-covered landscape was a stark but beautiful contrast to the familiar heat of Texas, and the views of the towering mountains, lush valleys, and glacier-filled bowls were awe-inspiring.

On that late August day in Washington State's Goat Rocks Wilderness, the temperature hovered around 37 degrees. As I made my way towards the notorious "Goat Rocks Knife Edge" traverse, I was filled with both excitement and nerves. This section of the Pacific Crest Trail (PCT) is renowned for being the highest and most perilous stretch in Washington. It's known for its severe exposure, with two steep, snow-packed scree slopes prone to rock falls and no shelter from storms for nearly a mile in either direction. The "Knife Edge" trail, named for its razor-thin, spine-like structure, presented a daunting challenge.

As I approached the Knife Edge, I found myself slipping and sliding on the packed snow. Through experience, I had learned that in situations where losing traction was a risk—whether due to loose gravel or snow—it's better to initiate the slide yourself rather than waiting for it to happen unexpectedly. Waiting can result in an uncontrolled slide and a more dangerous fall. By anticipating and initiating the slide, I had more control over the situation, even though complete control was never guaranteed.

As I continued along the snowy section, the trail transformed into a landscape of flat, loose rocks, surrounded by dense fog. The scene felt otherworldly, as if I had stepped onto a different planet. The wind picked up significantly as I began the ascent along the Knife Edge, reaching elevations from 6,900 feet to 7,100 feet. The thin, exposed trail, combined with the biting wind, made the climb both physically and mentally taxing. The thought of encountering a storm in this exposed terrain was particularly terrifying, as there was no protection whatsoever.

At this high elevation, I felt as though I might need to crawl along the trail to avoid sliding off either side of the mountain. My trekking poles offered minimal security against the harsh conditions. My hands and legs grew increasingly cold, prompting me to seek shelter behind a rock to retrieve my gloves and pants. Despite donning these layers, my hands remained freezing. A mountain goat appeared suddenly, leaping onto the trail and staring at me before disappearing into the fog. Unfortunately, my numbing hands prevented me from capturing this remarkable sight on camera.

Descending the mountain was a relief. The cold wind and treacherous conditions had taken a toll on me, and I knew I wouldn't meet my planned mileage for the day. Exhausted but hopeful, I consulted my map and discovered a campsite just 0.6 miles ahead. I filled up on water at a nearby stream and hiked the remaining distance to the campsite. The feeling of escaping the wind and settling into my tent was immensely comforting. As I sipped hot chocolate in my warm sleeping bag, I listened to the howling wind outside and felt grateful for the shelter I had found.

The experience of navigating such challenging conditions on the trail offered a valuable lesson in leadership: the importance of being proactive rather than reactive. On the trail, anticipating the possibility of sliding on snow or loose gravel and initiating the slide myself gave me more control over the situation. This principle of proactive versus reactive management is equally crucial in leadership.

Many leaders fail to apply this proactive mindset because they are not sufficiently engaged with their teams. To lead well, you have to understand what your team is dealing with, and the only way to know that is to actually be involved and paying attention. Leaders who aren't engaged usually don't see problems until they've already blown up. To be proactive, leaders must first be aware of potential issues by building strong relationships with their team members. This involves spending time with them, listening to their concerns, and understanding their roles and perspectives.

When you're engaged, you can spot problems early and head them off. If a team member is struggling or unhappy, a good leader sees it and goes talk to them about it. The bad version is waiting until they hand in their notice and then throwing money at them to stay. Stay in front of it.

In the workplace, just as on the trail, it is essential to anticipate and manage potential issues rather than waiting for them to become major problems. Being proactive allows leaders to handle situations more effectively and maintain a more stable and motivated team. By fostering strong relationships and staying engaged, leaders can better anticipate challenges and navigate them with greater control, leading to more successful outcomes for both the team and the organization.

CHAPTER 23
ENJOY YOUR JOY

Hiking and camping in cold rain for several consecutive days can be an arduous and often miserable experience, even for seasoned adventurers. After traversing over 2,000 miles through every kind of challenging condition you can imagine, one would think that such experiences would mentally prepare us for anything nature throws our way. Recently, I met a fellow hiker named Decaff, and we quickly bonded over our shared struggles with the relentless rain and fog. The absence of beautiful vistas during those dreary days made it increasingly difficult to keep our spirits high. The occasional stunning view was often our only relief from the persistent gloom.

As we neared the town of Trout Lake, Decaff mentioned that a local church was offering free rides into town. The prospect of avoiding the need to hitchhike was a huge relief, lifting a significant weight off our shoulders. The church had scheduled rides for 8:30 a.m. and 10:30 a.m. the following day. Given the location of my campsite, I realized I could easily catch the 10:30 ride, so I planned to leave by 5:00 a.m. Considering the challenging terrain, I conservatively estimated my pace at 2 miles per hour but remained optimistic about reaching the pickup point in time.

That morning, as I packed up my gear, excitement bubbled within me at the prospect of heading into Trout Lake for breakfast. After days of enduring cold and wet conditions, the thought of indulging in pancakes, bacon, and hot coffee was incredibly motivating. My love for hiking and nature was profound, but the allure of a warm, hearty meal had become one of my true joys on this journey.

As I hiked swiftly, I soon realized that I might actually make the 8:30 ride instead. My pace surged with adrenaline as I powered up the mountains, despite the early morning light barely breaking through the rain. Sweating and energized, I reached the designated pickup area at 8:15 a.m., where I found three other hikers eagerly waiting for the impending journey.

The church driver, a friendly local volunteer, transported us to a picturesque church that seemed to have emerged from a storybook. The immaculate white structure, framed by tall green trees, featured a covered area complete with picnic tables, electronics charging stations, and clean porta-potties. Remarkably, they allowed hikers to camp for free, showcasing their generosity and commitment to the hiking community.

Before unloading my damp gear, I made a beeline for the town restaurant, just a five-minute stroll through the quaint community. Known for their huckleberry pancakes, I decided to give them a try, and I was not disappointed! They were, without a doubt, the best pancakes I've ever had. Sitting outside with other hikers, we shared stories and chatted about the forecasted cold rain before heading back to the church.

Once back at the church, I laid out my damp gear to dry in the sunlight that had peeked through the clouds, seizing the opportunity to refresh my equipment. While I was busy setting everything up, the pastor came by to check on me as he worked outside. I expressed my heartfelt gratitude for their hospitality and marveled at the church's serene beauty. He kindly invited me inside, and as I stepped into the warmth, I was enveloped by the familiar "church smell"—a nostalgic scent reminiscent of my past visits to older houses of worship. We engaged in a meaningful conversation about biblical topics, which always rejuvenates my spirit, before I headed to the general store to pick up some supplies.

After collecting a few food items and plastic bags to keep my hands and feet dry, I took a refreshing nap on a picnic table, allowing the tranquility of the moment to wash over me. By lunchtime, a food truck specializing in delicious Mexican cuisine had set up outside the store. I couldn't resist grabbing a large burrito and a soda before returning to the church to eat my meal.

By the time I finished eating, my gear was dry, and it was nearly time for the 2:00 p.m. ride back to the trail. I packed up my belongings and made my way to the pickup area. The ride back included another hiker and a friendly golden retriever that reminded me fondly of my dog, Max, waiting for me back home.

My visit to Trout Lake proved to be incredibly productive. I enjoyed two fantastic meals, restocked my supplies, dried my gear, taken a great nap, charged my electronics, bonded with a dog, and engaged in a meaningful conversation with the pastor. As light rain began to fall again, stepping out of the warm car into the cold rain felt daunting, but I knew that the morale boost from my time in Trout Lake would help me power through the next stretch of the journey.

Finding joy in your life matters, especially when you're a leader. If you can't find some joy somewhere, you're going to turn into a cranky boss and your team will feel it. Joy can come from anywhere—a good meal, a real conversation, a hobby, a quiet moment. Whatever it is, hang on to it. It'll make you better at life and better at leading.

While finding joy outside of work is crucial, it's also important to derive joy from your role as a leader. Leaders can sometimes become so engrossed in the details and tasks of their jobs that they forget to appreciate the aspects that bring them joy. If you find yourself in a role that only brings misery, it's worth considering other options. Life is too short to spend in a leadership role that only brings unhappiness. Take some time to list the sources of joy in both your personal and professional life and make a concerted effort to cultivate that joy.

CHAPTER 24
NEVER QUIT ON A BAD DAY

Before I took on the challenge of thru-hiking the PCT, I watched countless YouTube videos about the adventure. One particular YouTuber, describing her journey on the Appalachian Trail (AT), mentioned an unspoken rule for long-distance hikers: "never quit on a bad day." During one of her tougher sections on the AT, she found herself stuck in her tent, waiting out cold, rainy weather. She looked miserable in the video—wet, tired, and cold. But as she described her experience, she emphasized that quitting on a bad day was something you simply couldn't allow yourself to do. Many people quit for legitimate reasons, such as injuries, excessive blisters, family emergencies, or illness, but deciding to quit just because you're having a tough time isn't wise. Watching that video stuck with me, and I was glad it did. I had many bad days on the PCT. Days when I felt tired, sore, hungry, frustrated, and overwhelmed by how many miles lay ahead of me. But none compared to one particular day, just north of Snoqualmie, Washington.

Snoqualmie is a small town located right off the PCT, about a half-mile walk from the trail. I planned to stop for breakfast, charge my electronics, and then head right back out to continue hiking. The restaurant, attached to a hotel, wasn't open yet when I arrived. So, I made myself comfortable in the hotel lobby, drank some of their coffee, charged my electronics, cleaned up in the restroom, and relaxed on a soft, comfy sofa by the fireplace. It was chilly outside that morning, and sitting on that sofa in front of the fire was a welcome reprieve. If I had walked into a hotel lobby back home in Texas looking and smelling like a dirty hobo, they would've likely asked me to leave. But here, they seemed accustomed to hikers and didn't bat an eye as several of us relaxed in their lobby. It was so warm and comfortable in there, especially with the cold weather outside, that I began considering staying. I hadn't planned on a "zero day," but with some other hikers talking about the cold, wet weather expected in the next 24 hours, the idea of staying in a hotel with a warm bed and hot bath was almost irresistible.

As tempting as it was to stay, I suppose it was fortunate that no rooms were available. It forced me to stick to my mileage plan, and after the restaurant opened, I enjoyed a warm meal of pancakes, bacon, and coffee. There's something about having a great meal in a warm, dry place that can lift your spirits. After breakfast, I gathered my gear, grabbed some snacks from a convenience store, and headed back to the trail. Upon reaching the trailhead, I met a fellow hiker named Camino. He was a 67-year-old with a grumpy disposition, and while we exchanged a few words about the weather, I quickly realized I didn't want to hike with him. I oriented myself on the trail and took off at a brisk pace, hoping to put some distance between myself and the cranky hiker.

For the next several hours, I maintained a strong pace before stopping for lunch. It was cold and windy up on the mountain, but I found a spot nestled between rocks and trees that shielded me from the wind. There, I enjoyed the convenience store cheeseburger, chips, and candy bar I had picked up earlier. Sitting alone, overlooking the beautiful mountains, I knew I would miss these moments once I returned to the "real world." As challenging as the PCT was, with all its physical and mental demands, the beauty, peace, solitude, and daily satisfaction of overcoming obstacles were things I knew I'd miss. I knew that once I finished the trail, I would long to be back out here, even on the tough days.

As I pressed on, the trail led me across a rocky ridge at the top of the mountain. The wind had been relentless, and although I had been fortunate to avoid rain so far, I saw a large white cloud slowly rolling in from behind the mountain. Having hiked in Washington for a while, I knew exactly what that meant—my dry conditions were about to vanish. Sure enough, the drizzle started and stuck with me for the remainder of the hike. By late afternoon, the drizzle had turned into a light rain, and the temperature continued to drop. When I finally reached my campsite as darkness set in, my feet and hands were soaked. The rain had slowly seeped through my gloves, socks, and shoes, leaving me cold and wet.

Setting up camp, I took extra care to keep my sleeping bag dry, storing it in a trash bag inside my pack. No matter how wet my other gear got, I knew I had to protect my sleeping bag and sleeping clothes. After getting everything set up, I climbed into my tent and changed into the only dry clothes I had left. I decided to string a line across the inside of my tent to hang my wet clothes, hoping they would dry out overnight. Big mistake. I had essentially been sleeping in a cloud, and the moisture seeped into my tent, making my clothes even wetter by morning.

At 4:00 a.m., I sat in my tent listening to the cold rain pound against the fabric. I had 25 miles to cover that day, and I was filled with dread. I couldn't summon any positivity that morning. It took everything I had just to say my morning prayer and start getting dressed. I found a pair of damp socks from a couple of days ago and put them on, followed by plastic grocery bags over my feet to keep them dry. I did the same for my gloved hands, layering plastic bags over them. I knew the day ahead would be miserable, but there was no avoiding it—I simply had to do it.

Once I packed up my gear and headed out into the cold, foggy, rainy conditions, it became clear this wasn't one of those times when things turned out to be "not as bad" once you got started. It was every bit as bad as I had anticipated. The first five miles of the trail were nothing but flat, loose, slippery rocks, and the thick fog made it almost impossible to see. My pace was barely half a mile per hour, and I quickly realized that making 25 miles was going to be nearly impossible. I even wandered off the trail at one point and found myself at the tent of Camino, the grumpy hiker, who grumbled, "this is not the trail." His mood was as bad as the weather.

That day was by far the worst of the entire hike. I remember telling myself that if a helicopter appeared offering to take me off the trail if I quit, I would've taken it. But no helicopter appeared, so I kept trudging along, repeating the YouTuber's advice: "never quit on a bad day." I could have turned back to Snoqualmie, checked into a hotel, and found a ride to the nearest airport to head home, but I chose to press on. As I had often told myself during dark, cold mornings in the desert, "the sun will shine again very soon," and it always did. While the sun didn't literally shine that day, the rain eventually stopped, the fog lifted, and the terrain improved.

"Never quit on a bad day" is not profound wisdom. It's a simple mindset, but it carried me through many tough days on the trail. Whether I was hiking through the heat of the desert, battling extreme winds in Tehachapi, dealing with shin splints, or choking on smoke in Northern California, that mantra stayed with me. It's the same advice I offer to leaders: don't quit on a bad day. Bad days are inevitable in leadership, but if you've led with character, work ethic, honesty, discipline, confidence, humility, and love, the sun will shine again. The bad days will pass, and the scars you earn along the way will make you a stronger leader.

Sometimes, knowing a bad day is coming can be the hardest part. It can make you want to avoid the challenge altogether. But when that happens, you simply have to start. That morning in my tent, I didn't want to begin the 14-hour day of misery, but instead of thinking about how tough the day would be, I just focused on each individual step—praying, drinking my coffee, doing my stretches, getting dressed, packing my gear, and walking. Avoiding the challenge wouldn't make it go away. When a task seems overwhelming, the most important thing is to START. There are plenty of valid reasons for a hiker to quit, but quitting due to a few bad days wasn't an option for me. As a leader, I encourage you to have the same mindset. When bad days come, remember that the sun will shine again soon, and you'll emerge stronger for having endured them.

CHAPTER 25
NEGATIVE NANCY

The Washington section of the PCT remains etched in my memory as perhaps the most beautiful part of the trail. However, I will also never forget how challenging and miserable it was at times. One particular morning, I found myself sitting under a tree, soaking wet, seeking even the smallest bit of shelter from the relentless rain. I was taking my usual 9:00 a.m. coffee and Pop-Tart break when I saw the cranky hiker, Camino, walk past me. Luckily, I was about 30 feet off the trail, and like most hikers in that miserable rain, he had his head down and didn't see me. I was already cranky and miserable and certainly didn't need to hear his constant complaining.

Once I finished my break, which did little to improve my mood, I hit the trail hard. I needed to cover about 22 miles that day to reach a campsite that would set me up for an easy hike into town the following day, but I was already behind schedule. With the challenging conditions and my slower-than-usual pace, it looked like I wouldn't make it to camp until about 8:00 p.m., which didn't exactly boost my motivation.

After a couple of hours, the rain finally stopped as I approached an old bridge spanning a deep, beautiful canyon.

Three hikers were on the bridge taking a break, their gear strewn over the railing, hoping to dry it out. I was incredibly jealous—getting a chance to dry your gear was a luxury at this point. As I paused on the bridge to take in the view, I overheard them discussing an upcoming alternate route that would shave about eight miles off the trail. I hadn't known about this alternate route, but once I heard them, I checked the Guthook app and found it.

I wasn't in the habit of seeking out shortcuts, but on this day, I was more than willing to make an exception. The comments on the Guthook app warned that the alternate route was tough and involved fording a small river, but it would definitely save time. As I was reading the comments and making mental notes, I overheard a couple nearby arguing. He was frustrated with her negative attitude, telling her that the whole group was tired of her constant negativity. He said, "We're all cold, wet, sore, and tired. But we make a plan and hike through it the best we can. Constantly complaining and being overly dramatic doesn't help anyone."

He sounded a bit harsh, but I understood his frustration. Once I finished eavesdropping, I headed down the alternate route with a greatly improved morale. Knowing I now had a shot at reaching my campsite by about 5:00 p.m. was a huge boost to my attitude. Within about two miles, I came to the river crossing mentioned in the app. It didn't look too challenging, but just on the other side was Camino, the old curmudgeon. He was trying to shout something at me as I took off my Hokas and socks and put on my Crocs to cross the river, but I couldn't hear him.

As I forded the cold river, using my trekking poles to brace myself against the strong current, I found myself dreading the likelihood of being stuck with Camino for the rest of the day. Once I crossed, I started drying my feet and putting my shoes back on while Camino complained that the alternate trail wasn't on the Guthook app. The lack of a mapped trail meant we'd have to trust the comments and hope it would lead us back to the PCT. Camino had a real problem with this and was about to re-cross the river and return to the original trail. However, my good mood and confidence in the alternate route convinced him to stick with me.

The first few miles with Camino weren't too bad. The trail was fairly easy, and I learned that he was 67 years old, had recently lost about 150 pounds, and was newly married. I also got to hear him complain about his job of over 20 years, which he claimed was full of incompetent people. As the trail became more challenging, the complaints started pouring out. He grumbled about contacting the PCT administration to complain about the condition of this trail, even though it was an alternate route he had chosen to take. His faith in the trail was quickly dwindling, and he even said, "I should have turned back like I originally wanted to instead of listening to you."

The trail was becoming very difficult, and my own faith was wavering, but Camino's constant negativity made it much worse. He didn't have to come with me—it was his choice. I wanted to tell him to either turn back or stop complaining. His negative attitude was dragging me down, and we were too far into the alternate route to turn back now. Complaining about things we couldn't control wasn't doing us any good. I just wanted to put my head down and power through.

Eventually, we came to a very steep incline, and I took off like a rocket, knowing Camino couldn't keep up with me on that climb. My legs and lungs were burning from the pace I set, but I was determined not to slow down and let him catch up. It worked like a charm! Part of me felt bad for leaving him behind, but I couldn't stand to be around him any longer. After powering through a few more miles in blessed silence, I was slightly concerned about whether this trail would lead me back to the PCT. Then, I came to a great camping spot just a few feet from the PCT. I had made it back to the original trail!

I set up camp, started making dinner, and watched Camino walk past without saying a word. I don't think he was very happy that I left him behind.

I once heard a great leadership quote in the movie "Remember the Titans." In one scene, an actor says, "Attitude reflects leadership." That quote resonated with me the moment I heard it, and it has always stuck with me. Leaders must inspire those they lead, and there is no way to inspire anyone with a negative attitude that repels people. Both Camino and the overly dramatic girlfriend in this scenario created an atmosphere of frustration and stress. This kind of environment makes it an uphill battle for anyone attempting to lead a group. Just as I wanted to distance myself from Camino, your team will want to distance themselves from you if you create a similar atmosphere.

As a leader, your goal is to cultivate a culture where your team wants to follow you. They should feel drawn to you and have a natural tendency to follow. When things get tough, as they inevitably will, they need to trust you as their leader. And there's no way to earn that trust if you've fostered a negative, high-stress culture.

Have you ever heard the term "herding cats"? If you know anything about cats, you know that trying to herd them would be nearly impossible. You'd spend all your time chasing a bunch of crazy cats and never make any real progress. Unfortunately, that's exactly what many "bosses" do. I put "bosses" in quotation marks to emphasize the difference between a boss and a leader. These bosses end up chasing stray cats and putting out fires, but they never truly lead because no one wants to follow them. Then they wonder why they never achieve the results they desire.

I often sit back in amazement and wonder how they don't see that they are the problem. Imagine two identical businesses: in one, you have a calm, encouraging, positive leader; in the other, you have a negative, overly dramatic leader. Which business do you think will be more successful? As you observe the culture and attitude of your team, it's crucial to consider the quote, "Attitude reflects leadership." The attitude or culture of your team is a direct reflection of you, their leader.

CHAPTER 26
NO TREPIDATION

"I remembered that the real world was wide, and that a varied field of hopes and fears, of sensations and excitements, awaited those who had the courage to go forth into its expanse, to seek real knowledge of life amidst it's perils" – Charlotte Brontë

On a cold Monday morning, September 6th, at 7:00 a.m., I was about to start the final stretch into Canada. I went through my usual routine—coffee, breakfast, Bible study, stretching, pushups, and packing up my gear—but a lot of mixed emotions kept hitting me. It was hard to believe the whole thing was almost over. I felt sad and excited at the same time, and a lot of memories from the trail kept running through my head.

Thinking back on the months leading up to this trip, I could see how much I'd changed. I went from "I would like to hike the PCT someday" to "I am going to hike the PCT no matter what." That shift took a lot of time and thought. A trip like this costs a lot of time, energy, and money, and it puts a lot of strain on your relationships. Once I decided, there was no room for second-guessing.

Now, standing on this beautiful morning just 20 miles from the Canadian border, I had a clear plan. I aimed to hike to a campsite situated about 6 miles from the border, where I would set up camp for the night. The following day would see me making the final trek to the border. If all went according to plan, I could return to Harts Pass by early Wednesday morning and hopefully catch a ride to Seattle in time for my Thursday morning flight. However, I felt a twinge of anxiety at the back of my mind, wishing I had given myself more cushion in my schedule to avoid the stress of potentially missing my flight.

I paused at a picturesque waterfall to refill my water supply and take in the beautiful view. It was an amazing feeling to know that the beautiful mountains I was starring at, was Canada. I was standing atop a Washington mountain looking into Canada. What an amazing feeling! After spending some time soaking in the moment, I encountered another hiker who was also heading to the same campsite. He shared his plan to set up camp, hike to the border, and return. Inspired by this idea, I decided to follow suit, knowing it would make for a strenuous but rewarding 32-mile day—12 of those miles would be completed with a much lighter pack.

After reaching the campsite, I set up my tent and took only my pack with snacks and water as I headed toward the border. After already hiking 20 miles, I felt invigorated; the thrill of nearing the end fueled my spirit. With this plan, I could complete a long hike on Tuesday, giving myself the cushion I needed for my upcoming flight.

It was just after 6:00 p.m. as I calculated my pace. With the lighter load, I estimated I could average around 3 miles per hour, allowing me to return to camp by approximately 10:00 p.m. While I accepted that my sleep would be minimal, I was more than willing to make the sacrifice for this moment.

As I made my way toward the border, my thoughts buzzed with a whirlwind of emotions—excitement, sadness, the challenges I had faced, and the amazing hikers I had met along the way. Less than a quarter mile from the Northern Terminus Monument, a surge of anticipation washed over me. Approaching the monument at mile 2,652.6, I stopped and just took it in. I had made it—alone, without any fanfare. Taking a moment to kneel, I expressed my gratitude to God for guiding me through this journey. I then stepped over the border, captured a little happy dance on video, snapped a quick picture atop the monument, and began my journey back to camp. The hike back to the campsite was exhausting! As I made my way through the dark, I felt like a zombie stumbling along the trail as I closed in on finishing the 32 mile day. I eventually made it back to my camp by about 10:30 p.m. and quickly fell into a deep sleep.

Taking on a leadership role is no small feat; it is a long, arduous journey that profoundly affects the lives of others. Leaders must exercise due diligence, making decisions without flinching. This entails seeking advice from trusted friends, family members, co-workers, or anyone who can provide honest and constructive insights. For those who are spiritually inclined, prayer can be a powerful source of wisdom and guidance.

If you take on leadership half-hearted, you're setting yourself up to fail. The job requires your full commitment.

When you're offered a leadership role, take it seriously. Park your ego at the door. Leadership isn't about you looking good; it's about guiding and supporting other people. Do your homework on what the role actually requires. Take an honest look at your own strengths and weaknesses, and how they fit the job. Talk to people you trust who will tell you the truth. They'll see things in the role you might be missing.

Once you've done that work and you're ready to decide, jump in with both feet. Don't take the role and then hold back. Bring enthusiasm and dedication and give it everything you've got. Leading people, like hiking the PCT, is a long, hard road. There will be hard days and there will be growth. Take all of it. Every challenge is a chance to get better.

Leadership, like a long hike, takes perseverance and the right attitude. The same way I had to deal with weather and terrain on the PCT, you'll deal with obstacles and setbacks in leadership. With determination and the right mindset, you'll get through them. Find the joy in the process itself. Be all in. Support your team and work to make a real difference.

As you start this leadership journey, take care of yourself and find some balance. Leadership is demanding, and if you don't take care of yourself, you can't lead well. Look for moments of joy and rest the way I did on the trail—the great views, the hot meals in town. Those are the moments that keep you going. Take it all in, and... happy trails!

CONCLUSION
THE JOURNEY CONTINUES

"*A mind that is stretched by a new experience can never go back to its original dimension.*" —Oliver Wendell Holmes

That quote really hits home for me, especially after finishing the PCT. A lot of people told me before I left that this hike would change me, and almost four years later, I know they were right. I'm not the same guy who started at the Mexican border. Coming back to what we call the "real world" has been hard. I put "real world" in quotes because I don't really buy that this is the real world. Chasing money to buy stuff we don't need, working ourselves to death for it, calling that life—that doesn't feel real to me. Most of us are running on a treadmill and don't even know it.

As I work through this transition, I'm realizing it's just another stretch of trail. The lessons the PCT taught me are the tools I use to figure out the next section. Coming home doesn't mean I have to fall right back into the same materialism and overstuffed calendar I was running from. My goal now is to take what I learned out there and apply it back here. Am I feeling buried and overwhelmed? Maybe I need a "pack shakedown." Am I forgetting to be grateful? Time to "appreciate the little things." Is life beating me up? "Trudging is inevitable."

The analogies from the trail fit my life right now just as well as they did out there. If I can pull this off, then the PCT won't have just changed me as a person—it will have changed how I live the rest of my life. I don't want this to be just a great memory I dust off and tell at dinners. I want it to keep paying off for years. The question I keep coming back to is: how do I take what I learned on the trail and actually use it in everyday life?

I recall a great group of hikers from Minnesota who embraced the PCT experience with open hearts. They never rushed to grind out miles, instead diving eagerly into every beautiful body of water they encountered, regardless of its chill. I vividly remember passing them on a particularly brisk day while they joyfully swam in an ice-cold lake, surrounded by shimmering snow. Rather than join them, I simply smiled, exchanged a few words, and continued on my path. In retrospect, I regret not seizing that moment, ignoring the discomfort of being cold, tired, wet, and the urgency to reach camp.

Days later, I conversed with this spirited group and shared my feelings of regret. They told me about their three simple goals: to finish the hike, to fully embrace every experience, and to enjoy one beer daily. A daily beer wasn't really my style, but I admired how carefree they were, and honestly, I was a little jealous. They got me thinking about how I do things. I often find myself highly organized and disciplined, yet I yearn to be spontaneous and adventurous. That tug-of-war shapes how I move through life.

The Minnesota group was a good reminder that it's OK to break the routine sometimes and let myself have fun. Going forward, I'm going to try to do that more often. The PCT really is a great metaphor for life. Every hiker takes the trail their own way, and the same is true for life. There's no one right way to do it. I just need to find a way to keep my disciplined side without losing the carefree side I found out there.

As I keep moving forward, I'm carrying what I learned from the Minnesota group and from the trail itself into the rest of my life. How you approach life shapes how you lead, and it shapes how you handle the hard parts. What I'm after now is a balance—keeping the discipline that's gotten me this far, but leaving room for spontaneity and adventure too.

The journey isn't over. I get to keep choosing to live a life that means something, and to be who I actually am. The PCT was a physical trek, sure, but it's an experience that will keep shaping me for the rest of my life. As I work these lessons into everyday life, I keep coming back to the same idea—real freedom isn't somewhere out there. It's in how you choose to live each day.

ACKNOWLEDGMENTS

I would first like to extend my deepest gratitude to Jesus Christ, for granting me the opportunity to embark on and complete such a journey. Without His guiding hand, I would never have been called to undertake this adventure, and I certainly would not have had the strength to see it through to the end. His divine presence was my constant companion, leading me through every challenge and triumph along the way.

To my two amazing kids, Landon and Madi, who have stood by my side through everything life has thrown at us, thank you. You have been there with me through every storm, with unwavering support. The pride I feel watching you both grow into the adults you've become gave me the fuel I needed to take on this hike. Your belief in me carried me through the hardest, darkest stretches of this trip.

Thank you also to my wife, Monique (Mo), who has put up with my rough transition back into the "real world" with more grace than I deserve. She has been my rock through a really pivotal stretch of my life. Her love and acceptance mean more than I can say. Her patience and understanding gave me the room I needed to find my footing again. She is also credited with the cover and author photographs.

I also want to extend my gratitude to my PCT hiking companion, River Stillwood— "Soul Sister"—whose gentle encouragement inspired me to embark on writing this book. I vividly recall her words, urging me to give myself permission to "be messy" as I began crafting the rough draft. Those words, like a soothing refrain, echoed through my mind, guiding me time and again when I needed them most.

Lastly, I want to remember my "Soul Dog" Max. You've been with me through many ups and downs in my life and we've had some great adventures together. I'll take a piece of you with me on all my future journeys.

Looking back on this whole journey, I'm filled with gratitude for the love and support I had behind me. The words of encouragement I received through social media from friends and family kept me going through some very challenging times. This adventure wasn't just a test of physical endurance. It was a reminder of the power of faith, family, and love. Every step I took was carried by the grace of God, the pride of my kids, the encouragement of friends and family, and the support of my wife. Together, they are the foundation that this whole journey was built on, and for that I am forever grateful. Thank you!

ABOUT THE AUTHOR

DAVID WILSON, ORIGINALLY from Konawa, Oklahoma, now calls Ft. Worth, Texas, home, where he lives with his wife, Monique. He is fortunate to live close to his children, Landon and Madi, and his new granddaughter, Quinn. With a career rooted in leadership within the hospitality industry, David is always on the lookout for new adventures to embark upon in his free time.